BJ 1251 .W66 1973

Woodson, Leslie H., 1929-

A view from the cornerstone

G. Allen Fleece Library
COLUMBIA INTERNATIONAL UNIVERSITY
7435 Monticello Road
Columbia, SC 29230

a view from the cornerstone

484 3

a view from the cornerstone

Leslie H. Woodson

MOODY PRESS :: Chicago

LP494 521

© 1973 by
The Moody Bible Institute
of Chicago

ISBN: 0-8024-9160-X

All rights reserved

The use of selected references from various versions of the Bible in this publication does not necessarily imply publisher endorsement of the versions in their entirety.

Scripture quotations from *The Living Bible* (Wheaton, Ill.: Tyndale, 1971) are used by permission of the publisher.

Printed in the United States of America

001311

Contents

Preface

NO BOOK should be written without a clearly defined raison d'etre. At this point the author is especially grateful, since not one but three reasons commanded his consideration. First, the Christian community has become lax in defining and defending the absolutes by which the faithful must live. Second, in the midst of overwhelming confusion within the household of faith, I have found it necessary to reevaluate and reaffirm my own priorities. I find that the institutional church increasingly does not speak for me in these matters. There is no better way to clarify one's head in a world of religious fog than by the discipline of writing out what he holds to be convictions worth living or dying for. Third, Leslie H. Stobbe, Editor of Moody Press, offered encouragement for me to pursue this endeavor. It was he who really fanned the latent spark into an open flame. To him I am indebted for the push which moved my pen to put my priorities into writing.

In addition, my gratitude must be expressed to the people of my local parish for their patience and support during the time-consuming task of writing. To my wife, Betty, I owe a debt of thanks for her understanding during those many evenings at home when I wanted to write and she wanted to talk. Our children, too, have been denied time and attention deserved from a father. They are a great troop, and I am sobered by their longsuffering with me. No little amount of personal appreciation should go to the publisher, whose patience in reading this manuscript and editing it for print is marvelous to behold. And, of course, to God our heavenly Father, whose great mercy and love have been so close to me throughout this writing, I owe my very life.

LESLIE H. WOODSON

Introduction

LIVING AT LOOSE ENDS leaves one with an uneasy feeling of slippery fluidity which totally obliterates the sense of stability and permanence so essential to a meaningful existence. In other words, a man has to be sure about something—sure enough to tie a knot in the end of his mental rope. Unless he does, everything will keep slipping through his fingers or, to stay with the analogy, through his mind. Everyone needs an open mind, lest he grow stale and brittle. But it should not be locked open at both ends so that the mental machinery is incapable of retaining anything at all. By the same token, it must be alert enough to throw out undesirable entries before they have a chance to turn the brain into a second-class flophouse.

We have been brainwashed to believe that a closed mind is never a good thing. The airy-brained connoisseurs of every new thought would have us believe that people with closed minds are bigoted, narrow, intolerant, prejudiced, and ignorant. Admittedly, one must be careful about shutting the mental gate too soon; but that it be closed and bolted sometime somewhere is a must. Any man who leaves his head and heart continually open to every transient idea that comes along will become a candidate for hell or the insane asylum, or both.

Few people are able to believe strongly in anything anymore. Nothing is clearcut for contemporary man. Right and wrong are relative matters and must be determined by the situation. Ethics and morals are never absolute; they are contextual. In most instances it is practically impossible to know for sure what one should do when faced with a choice between moral alternatives. Guidelines by which an earlier generation lived are no longer valid. White is now a dull gray, and black is similar enough to be indistinct. This means that just about everything is acceptable in certain circumstances, and the circumstances are usually arranged quite conveniently.

To put it another way, priorities are as scarce as albino blackbirds! Hardly anyone thinks of putting any conviction or principle in a permanent and inviolable position. What is sacred today may be ridiculously naïve tomorrow, just as yesterday's sanctities are today's humorous examples of religious superstition. There is nothing to be found anywhere in the world that deserves first place for time and eternity in any person's life, according to modern mentality. The only thing the secular man is absolutely sure of is that there are absolutely no absolutes. He has been told this by educators, philosophers, behaviorists, ethicists, jurists, and theologians. The man on the street finds it foolish to disagree with such an array of informed and respected world spokesmen.

This new era, "the age of Aquarius," was at first a welcome thought. It was to be a period of freedom and permissiveness, a time of abandoning old-fashioned codes of right and wrong. At last man could feel free to be and do whatever he honestly considered to be right in any given circumstance. Gradually it is dawning on him, however, that living by a subjective code puts far more responsibility on him than the older social regimentations. And the heavy responsibility is more than the average man can bear. Either he throws off the weight and descends into degeneracy, or he struggles under it until the resulting chaos becomes more burdensome than the traditional standard.

Man's idea of utopia is a free society. Something within the spirit of humanity demands freedom for the individual.

This stems from the divine risk that permitted Adam to choose. With freedom to choose comes responsibility for the choice. Such responsibility is borne out in the aftermath of Adam's misuse of his God-entrusted power to decide for himself. And the story, ever-repeating like a tune on a broken phonograph record, is seen in the lives of countless people today. They have found their freedom too demanding.

Today's young people, reared in a permissive culture where there are hardly any prohibitions and where punishment is extremely lenient, have discovered that their easy-come-easy-go world is less than satisfying. It is the seasoned judgment of growing numbers of both parents and psychologists that our youth are rebelling against this undisciplined life. Society must accept its role of enforcing guidelines on its citizens for the protection of the individual himself as well as the citizenry at large. A system of values must be devised, by which persons can gauge their self-actualization under God and their acceptance or rejection by their fellows.

While society must fulfill its role as a parent body which loves, protects, and disciplines its sons, man is ultimately responsible for his own priorities. He alone must establish these priorities, since no law enforcement can be successful without individual respect for the supreme value of existence. The laws of society draw attention to what is wrong and right. They provide no power for obedience any more than did the decalogue in Paul's day. Something inside man must do that. Innate human decency helps, but it is not enough. And it is at this point that we confront the place of the Christian faith in man's potential for creative living.

Life either has no significance at all or is too important to be lived at loose ends. A person's concept of human existence can be quickly perceived by watching his behavior. His motives for action, his methods of implementing dreams, and his ultimate goals all are the logical outcome of a basic philosophy. What is man? Why is he here? Where is he going?

Do his actions make any difference? Is he ultimately responsible to the Creator-God? If so, what does that responsibility entail? These are only a few of the provocative and haunting questions which disturb us.

If one is a materialist, his goal is to accumulate as much of this world's goods as possible. Others often are ruthlessly trampled if they happen to get in the way. Of course, the one doing the trampling is apt to be trodden under boot as surely as anyone else. Persons holding a materialistic philosophy bow before no other shrine. Yet, how completely unsatisfying it is.

Arthur Miller's play, *The Death of a Salesman,* is an example of this. Willy lived his entire life in a dream world where success was always just around the corner. But it never arrived. All the while, Willy kept pretending, refusing to face the tragic reality of his situation, which worsened daily. Finally, fired by his employer, he killed himself in order to allow his wife to collect his insurance. At least his family would think of him with some sense of respect when they collected twenty thousand dollars. In those tender moments toward the end of the play, as she kneels by his new grave, Linda says softly to herself, "He only needed a little salary." To which Charlie, lifelong friend of Willy, replies, "No man needs *only* a little salary." And we might add, "nor does he need *only* a big salary!" But, for the materialist, that about sums it up. That is his priority in life.

A person's values always will determine what he considers to be important, whether he is an atheist, a communist, a humanist, or whatever. A Muslim denies himself many of the pleasantries of the present world in order that he may have them in the next. The Buddhist shapes his whole life by a suppression of all desire as a preparation for Nirvana, or "desirelessness." A Hindu is careful to revere every living thing because he believes that reincarnated souls inhabit bodies of animals and insects. Such philosophies determine priorities which shape one's earthly existence.

What personal priorities should grow out of a Christian philosophy? What do we hold to be self-evident in the area of ultimates? When all the frills of earthly life are cut away and we get down to the bare essentials of Christian existence, what is left? Jesus stated it concisely when He challenged us to seek first the kingdom of God and His righteousness with the promise that "all these things shall be added unto you" (Mt 6:33). Although no one who loves and trusts the Lord cares to question this simple admonition, it is not very specific. We are prone to ask what is "the kingdom of God," and how are we to know just what "his righteousness" consists of. Without specific clarity, our concept of that which is basic may be divorced from the Christian ethic.

There is only one way to ascertain what Jesus meant by seeking the kingdom of God *first*. That is by subjecting this particular statement to the penetrating light of the whole of His ministry. The attitude He had and the response He made to church and state, righteous and sinful, friend and foe, God and Satan interpret the word about priorities as the Master conceived them. Therefore, our purpose shall be to distill from the whole of Scripture and ecclesiastical doctrine derived from it (though the latter source is far less important than the former) the pure and unadulterated essence of Christian living. In the following pages we shall set ourselves to the difficult task of peeling away the many layers of tradition and cultural accretions which have covered the core of truth. If we can get at its heart, it will be discovered that the fundamental pattern of living that typified Jesus and the early disciples was far less complex than is sometimes thought.

As we read the New Testament, there is the feeling that the apostles seldom had to wrangle over decisions involving their personal priorities. They did meet together for worship and fellowship, and they must have discussed all kinds of issues. A great conference was called in Jerusalem to decide what grounds were necessary for admitting Gentiles into the church. But this was a communal decision, not a matter of personal priorities. At times they were impulsive in their confrontation of life's exigencies. They made some serious blunders, but they were so dedicated that their rashness in making judgments seems to have been offset by their enthusiastic loyalty. They were unencumbered by denominationalism and theological schools where side issues often become much too important and center stage is overlooked for some cheap penny arcade.

If the disciples of the first three centuries were living in our technocratic world of automation, crime, dope, and cultic frenzy, how would they act? Would they find it harder to make decisions, or would their few cardinal priorities guide them now as effectively as long ago? Better still, what would Jesus do in a world like ours—a world all mixed up about values, morals, virtue, ethics, and change? Is there reason to believe that He would alter His way of looking at life if He had to face our complex world? Or would He tear away the complicated facade of our sophistication and point once again to the utter simplicity and stark seriousness of life under the surveillance of the heavenly Father? The latter possibility is the more reasonable of the two.

If we could know with certainty what Jesus would do in every given situation, our problem of determining priorities would be over. We still would have the greater difficulty of *doing* what we know to be unequivocally right. But at least there would be no more arguing or debating issues, which takes up so much of our time and saps so much of our energies today. What we need is the mind of Christ that we may *know* what takes precedence over everything else. We also need the spirit of Christ that we may *do* what that imparted wisdom clearly demands. Therefore, with a prayer for success in our search, we embark on a dual quest—a quest for both a Christian mind and a Christian spirit.

To avoid formality, I shall dispense with the editorial *we*. It is my intention to share my own convictions, not those of a sectarian or provincial group, with you. In order to do that, I must bare my soul and expose my heart. At times such openness can be embarrassing, but the need to share is too great to worry about the risk of exposure. If this is to be an honest book, I must be frank. Where my failure to live up to my priorities is known to me, I shall try to say so. Pity the man who never sets his goals higher than his achievements. But pity also the man who acts as though he has come closer to reaching his goals than anyone else. God forbid that anyone will think that I am talking down to him. I stand on no pedestal from which to preach divine judgment on others. If there is judgment in these pages, it is judgment on myself as much as on anyone else. And that judgment comes not from me or you, but from God.

It is my opinion that we shall once again find personal peace and power if the priorities can be discovered and faithfully observed. Unless we become men and women of integrity, there can be nothing but disappointment and defeat, degeneration and death. In these pages I have made the effort to distinguish between right and wrong, good and bad by positing the rudimentary and fundamental guideposts by which such delineation can be made.

You must decide for yourself whether these unbending and inflexible priorities are valid. Every man must drive down his own stakes at those points where he senses the most caution and carefulness are required. What you and I both are compelled to do is make dead certain that those guideposts are driven deep in the very places where Jesus would plant them were He deciding the issues.

Setting up priorities is simply another way of discovering the will of God. One must know His will in order to establish what takes precedence in life, but one must also set up some priorities if he expects to discover the divine will. Do not get hung up on the procedure of which comes first. Rather, determine priorities on the basis of present understanding of God's will with the certainty that the divine plan will grow clearer as priorities begin to take shape.

1

Sacred and Secular

NO MAN CAN BEGIN to construct a framework of personal priorities until he has laid down a solid, supportive base. The more important the proposed edifice, the more attention given the underpinning. If one is putting up a tent, it may be needful only to find a dry spot of earth. If a garage is being built, more care is given to preparing the ground and pouring the concrete. But if the structure is a twenty-story high-rise, it is imperative that steel piles be driven deep into the earth and points of stress and strain be precisely determined.

Could anything be more important than the building of one's life? Only if a man thinks of his life as a brief frolic of frivolous futility can he disregard the base. Even then he is a loser, never a neutral nonparticipant in causes and consequences. If life is of value—and most people think it is, unless they have been disillusioned by some humanistic philosophy—it must be anchored to a firm support. Any life which is going to rise to heights of joyful fulfillment must first deepen its roots. A direct relationship exists between the height of one's life and the depth of his foundation. Every specific priority grows out of a more general and inclusive "priority of priorities." This is our underpinning, our roots, our foundation. This is what I call "a view from the cornerstone."

Very little progress can be made in this discussion until

we decide whether existence in this world is to be viewed as sacred or secular. My concern has nothing to do with the older usage of these terms by which the monastic order of life was distinguished from the kind of life that rubbed shoulders with the world outside. Our world makes it all but impossible to dwell in any kind of insulation which would render us supposedly uncontaminated. Rather the words *sacred* and *secular* describe two ways of looking at the world of which every man is a part. And he must choose between the two because no middle ground is open to him.

Although renunciation of worldliness as a way of life distinct from and contrary to Christlikeness is an obligatory facet of serving God, no one should feel constrained to renounce the world. Man is a part of the world, a part of its matter and its community. There is no way to change that, nor is there any reason why we should want to. It is not Satan who has given us life and placed us in this world, but God Himself. Our being here is His will, and there is no justifiable rationale for withdrawing from societal existence. Therefore, the farthest thought from our minds should be the type of detached aloofness that was characteristic of the Essenes of Jesus' time.

To see the earth and life upon it as sacred is to be aware that there is far more to this business of living than the tangible goods of this world or the seventy years allotted us to enjoy them. I never look at the material world without feeling that it is all a vestibule to a vastly greater dimension. Each time the sun peeps over the east rim and summons the beginning of a new day, it brings with it a growing certainty that this is just the prelude to something even more wonderful to come. Everything has the feel of being a part of the unfolding, divine drama, the end of which must be breathtaking in its eternal splendor.

To see the world as sacred means that "this is my Father's world," and that everything has everlasting value and meaning because He has made it and blessed it. Nothing is accidental, unplanned, or unscheduled. No matter what happens, it never surprises Him who is the beginning and the end of all things. Thus, to view the world as sacred means to put one's trust and confidence in something other than man and the things he can see and touch. It means that both world history and future destiny are perceived as being grounded in the divine Spirit responsible for the material universe and the metaphysical reality behind it. The psalmist had this sacred perspective when he penned, "It is better to take refuge in the LORD than to trust in man" (Ps 118:8, NASB), because, as this thought is amplified in another text, "His spirit departs, he returns to the earth; In that very day his thoughts perish" (Ps 146:4, NASB).

When man allows himself to be sensitive to the sacred nature of the created order, he becomes aware of the incomparable loveliness and exquisite beauty of everything that composes this human habitat. He observes the hand of a loving Creator who had man's well-being in mind when He designed His plan for all ages. Every detail of the world around us has a glory all its own. Nothing is drab, colorless, or void of purpose. We feel a deep kinship with all of life, and our actions are monitored by reverence for the entire universe.

Seeing our world through a focus of sacredness does something to our whole approach to living. What the older churchmen used to call "the fear of God" colors our total perspective. Through His creation He communicates with us, and in the midst of it we are made conscious of the spiritual Presence that hallows the commonplace. From the unfolding of a buttercup to the confirming of a business contract, there is something of the serendipitous, the exciting discovery of happy things in unexpected places. Mundane moments grow less common with the advancing years as the process of aging makes everything more beautiful, as though finishing touches are being added to that which has been created.

To see the world and life upon it in any other way is to have what may be called the secular view. I am using the word "secular" to describe a lifestyle which ignores the dimension of the spiritual, a way of life which acts as if God did not exist. The secularist ignores God because he believes either that God does not exist, or that if such a deity should be, He really does not matter. The secularist does not think of men and women as God's people, nor does he conceive of the earth as God's world. God makes little if any difference in the life of a thoroughgoing secularist. He may refer to God, but it will be in a different connotation than that given by the one who believes all of life to be sacred. Most of our astronauts have been awed by a deep and natural reverence as a result of their experiences in outer space. Some felt inclined to read the story of creation. The fact that others have flippantly affirmed that they did not find God "out there" says something about the lostness of man rather than the absence of God. And the fact that some have felt nothing of that awe but were prone to volatile profanity even on the moon points up the basic distinction to be made between the sacred and secular views.

Lately we are hearing more and more about the secular climate. Augustine's *City of God* has been replaced by Cox's *Secular City*. Secular man lives in a secular world, receives a secular education, engages in a secular occupation, embraces a secular philosophy, belongs to a secular church, and blends perfectly into a completely secular society. And it is from this restricted perspective that man's empty, hollow existence springs. The froth and frill which offers a temporary respite from the boredom and frustration of such a way of life is short-lived. In the long run it means nothing.

Luther was right when he suggested that there should be no distinction between sacred and secular. By this observation, however, the reformer did not mean that everything flows into a hazy, ambiguous world where everything is seen in a secular light. Rather, he insisted that all of life should be brought into a sharpened focus in which nothing is secular at all. For Luther, the whole universe and everything within it was sacred. This is precisely what I am affirming in these pages. We do not divide our existence into sacred and secular. Either we are secularists, or we see the whole of life as sacred.

The contrast between persons with sacred and secular outlooks should not be related to piety or lack of it. We should never permit ourselves to believe that all secular people are immoral and degenerate. Although secularity tends toward laxity of convictions about right and wrong, one can still find confirmed secularists who lead decent, disciplined lives. Secularism has more to do with where one finds his security than with whether or not he is morally lax. And this brings us back to the original premise that the foundation is *the* priority (general) which precedes priorities (specific).

Secularism is a style of living which dupes us into misconstruing means as ends. The material things of earth absorb our time and energy as if there were nothing beyond them. The earthly realm has meaning only as it is understood in its wider and more inclusive spiritual dimension. But that is not obvious to the secularist. This does not imply that we should neglect or ignore the world, but it does mean that we should carefully regard it as a doorway and not as a destination. Security may reside in man himself and in the tangible realities among which he dwells. Or it may be found in the awareness that something or Someone stands over and above him to work out His eternal plan in the individual's life. The first understanding of life is what I mean by the secular lifestyle. The later is that which I have been calling sacred.

Monasticism, in which the holy withdraw from contact with the present world order, is a form of religious hyperopia, or farsightedness. Whether in a walled-in monastery, or in a make-believe capsule subjectively constructed around one's mind, such is a one-world philosophy. Secularism, on the other hand, in which the person rejects anything except the world order as now known, is a kind of myopia, or nearsightedness. Nothing is really seen other than what is right before one's nose. This, too, is a one-world philosophy. Looking at life as sacred is the healthier visual approach. In this way one sees both worlds and keeps them in proper balance without slighting either.

John the Baptist might be suggested as an example of the monastic focus on the world. Without reflecting upon his valid prophetic ministry, it may be noted that his underlying motivation was a farsighted, one-world obsession. Judas Iscariot, to go to the other extreme, would exemplify the secular approach which is so shortsighted as to get hung up with the present order. That which distinguished Jesus' evaluation of life was not that He assumed a middle-of-the-road, ameliorating position between John and Judas. It was much more than that. Christ's perspective was due to the higher base on which He stood, and from which He saw a panoramic spread that included both the earthly and the spiritual, both the past and the future, both the human and the divine. Indeed, this kind of overview is not available to us as it was to Him who embraced the best of both worlds. But it is from Him that the Christian must take his clues as to where the supportive foundation is to be placed. Neither withdrawal from nor identification with the present world order is the stance for me. My base priority is a balanced involvement in both worlds with an acceptance of the ultimate as a prelude to and a determinant for the penultimate (the important but not final). That is what I mean by *sacred*. And that is where my own priorities as a Christian must begin.

If this book does what it is designed to do, it will be

clearly discernible that each of these specifics grows out of this view from the cornerstone. My presupposition sets the course for every confrontation with alternate ways of facing the particular issues. Often these issues are not drawn up in a manner which makes a decision simple or easy. Sometimes the available choices are not between right and wrong so much as between wrong and less wrong. This is because the Christian ethic is made for a Christian society, and we do not have that. Where there are practicing non-Christians or churchmen who are unchristian in their attitudes, these ramifications have to be considered. My pattern is to look at all sides of issues from this basic priority of life as sacred. The resulting decisions are then arrived at not so much by contextual relativism in specifics as by inflexible absolutism in the foundation for constructive Christian living.

Study Questions

1. What is meant by the expression "priority of priorities" as used in this chapter? How would you define your own ultimate priority? In what way does it differ from the author's?
2. Explain the difference between renunciation of the world and renunciation of worldliness. Can you think of any Scriptures which help to clarify this distinction?
3. Is it possible to compartmentalize life into part sacred and part secular? Explain your answer.
4. What is meant by "balanced involvement"? How does that expression describe a view of life which might be called *sacred?*

2

Christ or Cause?

MAN IS ALWAYS LOOKING for a cause to which he can give his energy and support. Something within him demands union with a larger interest. Born to live in community, every person has a compelling drive to identify with some group espousing a particular concern which gives life an objective. Usually such a nucleus of people with a common dedication can be found with little or no trouble at all. Thousands of causes, some small and some large, solicit the support of the populace at large. They run the gamut from the local society for the preservation of community archives to the United Nations, from the volunteer fire department to the organizations for stopping our involvement in foreign wars, and from the supporters of a local option to the Gideons International. No one needs to hunt for a cause if he has enthusiasm to offer.

At times we find someone who is a do-it-yourself loner who mounts his soapbox and starts a cause of his own. This is the way many of our better-known interest groups got their start. And no time in history has lent itself more readily than the present to new fads and persons to vocalize them. Surely there is nothing which any of us could dream up that somebody else has not already made into a fetish and gathered a few people to make noise about.

Not all causes are good. Of course, not all are bad either.

Some are just plain silly—even stupid. Enormous amounts of energy and effort are wasted every day by people devoted to causes which are not worthy of their intelligence. Many give themselves to such causes without careful thought. Often their fanatical allegiance comes from being duped into the adoption of a false sense of values. Others do it in spite of their knowledge that the entire thing is ludicrous. They do it just for the sake of doing it. And that carefree, irresponsible attitude develops out of a lack of established priorities in a world where men have been taught that existence itself is meaningless.

Many of the rabid and violent acts of mobs can be explained by the herd complex running wild without responsible leadership. These people get into the action without really knowing what they are supporting. If they knew, they might refrain from getting involved, but it is more exciting to be where the action is. So multitudes refuse to think seriously for fear their cause might not claim them.

Being a part of a movement gives the individual a feeling of strength and power. He finds his identity in the group and feels a sense of importance when he is accepted as a part of it. Without the cause which binds together persons of like interest, the individual thinks of himself as a nobody. Thus, causes stem from man's need for a social context small enough to handle, and society in turn creates causes to insure its preservation. Man is not a hermit. He must have society. And in that society there will be causes. That is inevitable.

We all admire people who espouse a legitimate cause and stick to it. No one likes a stubborn know-it-all, but one can be loyal to what he believes without acquiring that kind of reputation. We do not like the hard-nosed bigot, and we like the sponge-nosed softy no more. When a man really believes in a principle, a purpose, or a program, he should stand up and let the world know how he feels about it. Even if he is wrong, how will he ever realize it unless he is heard and challenged by an opposing view?

Christianity is a cause. The Christian church is made up of people who support the cause. Few people would argue that it is not a good cause. To be sure, there have been times when misguided zealots within the Christian community have done great damage in the name of religion. But those were exceptions to the rule. A more general picture is that of an organization which, ever since its beginning, has had in mind the betterment of man's earthly and heavenly lot. Men and women from all walks of life have given themselves unstintedly to endorsing and supporting the way of life propagated by the church.

Schools and hospitals, orphanages and nursing homes, hostels and social centers have been conceived and sponsored by men and women who believed in what the Christian church stands for. Even during those times when its voice has not been as strong as could be desired, having the church around has cultivated a degree of moral decency and has made persons who militate against decent atmosphere feel uneasy. Thoughts of living in a land where the Christian community is unknown leaves us shuddering with visions of indescribable horror.

Within Christianity there are various subgroups who rally around some particular facet of the faith which is held to be more important than the rest of Christendom understands. For this reason we have Roman Catholicism, Orthodoxy, and Protestantism. In the latter division is found an increasing number of denominations majoring in the same field but minoring in special interests. Added to this are still other groupings constructed around either a liberal or a conservative approach. This is evident in Catholicism as well as in Protestantism. And, as if this were not enough, the community of faith within the more evangelical bodies is compartmentalized again into cells of people who cling to particular dogmas.

The last half of the twentieth century has witnessed a growing attempt on the part of more liberal fellowships to eliminate the organized segments in favor of an ecumenical community of faith. While the ecumenical spirit is always welcomed by true Christians, the concept of unification into one world church is not. For this basic reason, the conciliar movements are beginning to break apart. Diversity is a normal pattern of human existence, and the pattern is not changed by becoming a member of the Christian church. Denominationalism (an evil word for some) is not bad per se any more than is ecumenicity (also holding an evil connotation for some persons). Too much blame for the failure of the church has been placed on the use of different communal names. Rancor in the church is bad, but that is discovered within subgroups as well as between them. Christian competition probably is a necessary motivation for the mission of the church, since human life is geared to this kind of lifestyle both inside and outside the Christian community.

It must be agreed that our problem is not due to our division into groups, subgroups, or subsubgroups. Every man has his special concerns and should be entitled to them. Naturally he will be drawn for fellowship to those who share his penultimate interests. But he must recognize them as secondary, not primary. As long as this is the case, denominationalism will be no more a negative and divisive factor than that which exists in a corporation where several distinct departments pursue specific objectives to reach the general goal. We go wrong in the Christian church when we permit small causes to become ends rather than means to the all-inclusive purpose of God. They can easily become a major field instead of a minor interest.

When Paul wrote his initial letter to the Corinthians, he

pled with them "to stop arguing among yourselves. . . . to be of one mind, united in thought and purpose" (1 Co 1:10, Living Bible). Some insisted that they were disciples of Paul, or Apollos, or Peter. Others demanded recognition of their group as the only legitimate disciples of Christ. The apostle went into a long discourse about this unfortunate development and pointed out that, in spite of their particular interests, their ultimate priority was with Jesus Christ. To the Galatians, he exclaimed, "God forbid that I should boast about anything except the cross of our Lord Jesus Christ" (Gal 6:14, Living Bible).

Many people will fight for their own brand of Christianity—Catholic, Baptist, Methodist, Pentecostal—while not taking as strong a stand for Christ. One naturally wonders where their priority really is. Religious parties or denominations are only a means to an end. When anything religious gets in the way of being Christian, then the religious must take a back seat. It is Christ who died for me, forgave my sins, called me to preach, and gives me my reason for being. Therefore, my priority is not a cause—good as it may be—but a Person.

Taking a position which often is in total disagreement with the pronouncements of one's denomination is not easy, but it is imperative if one is to be faithful to what Christ commissioned him to be and do. No man has been called to go along with a program, but to take up his cross and follow a Person. At times the program is in line with what one understands that Person to want from him. Then the institutional design is a means to the end of glorifying Christ. But when that program conflicts with what an individual believes to be God's will for his life, he must refuse to comply with the religious orders. He can never do religious things as ends in themselves. He is not a secularist who *uses* religion for human ends. On the contrary, he sees life as sacred and thus rejects any prostitution of the ultimate divine objective.

A prime example of the clash which can come between Christ and a cause is found in the struggle of the ancient church with the institution of Jewry. When several of the apostles were arrested for proclaiming the gospel in the temple, it was Simon Peter who served as spokesman for the Christians before the infuriated Council of Jewish Fathers. His only justification for running counter to the established program of Judaism was stated in words easily understood by all: "We ought to obey God rather than men" (Ac 5:29). Jesus Christ had top priority that day in Jerusalem.

The Colossian epistle says we should live in such a way "that in all things he [Christ] might have the preeminence" (Col 1:18) or, as *The Living Bible* puts it, "he is first in everything." If the Lord is to be first in my life, then His word takes precedence over tradition or ecclesiastical pronouncements. When any question arises about decision making, the final criterion is what Jesus said about it. And if there is no clear word from Him about the isolated situation, my decision must be determined by the context of His life and deeds. I can never permit myself to become party to anything which would be out of keeping with His Spirit. Of course, where there is no clear word from Him regarding the issue at hand, I must allow difference of opinion on the part of other people. They must not be branded as unchristian because their decision is not mine. But, regardless of what others may do, my own judgment is to be directed by what I think Jesus would have done in a similar situation.

Causes come and go; Christ is "the same yesterday, and to day, and for ever" (Heb 13:8). When one becomes married to a cause, he takes the chance of being widowed. How many causes are now dead and forgotten except in history books—causes which were ardently supported by men who were certain at the time that they were identifying with a movement destined to be eternal? But as causes die, Christ is perceived more and more to be alive. Men try hard to keep their special interest groups alive, but they die anyway. Men tried hard to kill Christ once for all, yet He lives.

Paradoxical as it may appear, that is the way it is. Movements, even the greatest and most long-lived of them, are temporal. Only Christ is eternal. If there were no other reason for giving Christ personal priority, the durability of that choice would be logic enough.

Though men and women need causes in order to find their identities, even these identifying groups can contribute to one's lostness. People choose subgroups for personal extension of their concerns only to be disappointed by a depersonalization that devastates the human need for significance. This is because man is lonely even in a crowd. The smaller the crowd, the less lonely he may be; but what he needs to establish his identity is not a group so much as it is a partnership. It is only as he is joined to one other person in love and loyalty that identity is fully shared and understood.

Marriage is an illustration of this fulfillment of personhood. No marriage is a group. Communal marriages, with which some have experimented in our time, are disenchanting after a while. Two make a marriage. Any more than that destroys the meaningfulness in the identifying relationship. The coming of children creates a *family*, but they must not be allowed to be a part of the marriage. Parents are not married to their children. When that happens, nothing is left but chaos in the marriage itself. When my own wife died, I still had my three children. But they were a group of which I was a part, a cause which ranked at the top of my interests. Even with a cause like that, I was lonely.

Three is a crowd. Top priority cannot be given to a

crowd. It must be reserved for a person. In the context to which we have been referring, that Person is Christ. Paul was so completely right when he stated "at the name of Jesus every knee should bow, of those who are in heaven, and on earth, and under the earth, and that every tongue should confess that Jesus Christ is Lord, to the glory of God the Father" (Phil. 2:10-11, NASB). If Christ is Lord, as was the earliest creed of Christendom, then He has priority over all the the causes of earth. That includes those causes which carry with them some Christian brand. An old and familiar hymn says it well:

> There is a name I love to hear, I love to sing its worth;
> It sounds like music in mine ear, the sweetest name on earth.
> Oh, how I love Jesus, Oh, how I love Jesus,
> Oh, how I love Jesus, because He first loved me!
>
> FREDERICK WHITFIELD

Among the most recent causes to appear is what is popularly referred to as the Jesus movement. That which stands out about the young people in this movement is that they have only one allegiance. Their lives have been changed by the Saviour and, having tried everything else in vain, they are now convinced that there is only one way—Jesus Christ. Let us pray that their enthusiasm will not fade into another religious cause and finally run its course. It would be easy for the Jesus movement to become another "denomination" with is formalities and rituals, to solidify into a religious organization. Should such a tragedy befall this group, individuals within the movement will be forced to take issue with the cause in order to put Christ first.

One of the most exhilarating experiences ever to come to Simon Peter and his companions was that which transpired on the Mount of Transfiguration. In the midst of the heavenly luminescence emanating from the person of Jesus were seen Moses and Elijah conversing with the Lord. So overawed was Peter by the spectacle that he proposed the erection of a trinity of shrines on the mount, one for each of the holy men. Three great causes would thus be reinforced by a kind of syncretizing "federation of churches" representing the law, the prophets, and the gospel. But the divine voice put an end to all such speculation with the timeless mandate, "This is my beloved Son, in whom I am well pleased; hear ye him" (Matt. 17:5). Henceforth Peter, James, and John saw *Jesus only.* From that moment, by God's clear decree, Christ became the priority of their lives.

When all the viable options are examined, the causes weighed, and the movements evaluated, Christ is my choice above all. *Jesus only*—that is the label which I choose to carry. The first building block to be laid upon the life-assacred foundation is Jesus Christ. It is upon this that I base my view from the cornerstone.

Study Questions

1. It has been said that it is better for the job to seek the man than for the man to seek the job. Can this be said about a cause? Is it true?
2. Think of a current cause that you could not endorse. Why not? Is there a cause which you could support but do not? Are you justified in not giving it your support?
3. How does loyalty to a Person rather than a cause help to lessen the friction often felt in religious groups? How is friction increased by such loyalty?
4. Man chooses a cause for purposes of identification and personal extension. How is Christ the fulfillment of personhood in a manner in which no cause or movement can equal?

3

History and Experience

IT WOULD BE IMPOSSIBLE for me to overstress the necessity of maintaining a balance between the historical Christ of revelation and the contemporary Christ of experience. Among the weaknesses of the faith in modern times is the ultraconservative obsession with history and tradition without due regard to the mighty acts of God which happened since breakfast this morning. Another weakness, at the other extreme, is the ultraliberal concern with the God-in-process craze with little interest in what took place in Israel at the beginning of the Christian era. And although the theological orientation is vastly different for the evangelical, it is becoming an increasing problem among us to avoid the substitution of religious thrills for an historic-rooted commitment to the saving work of Christ.

Christian experience must keep close to the historical Christ-event which brought redemption to mankind. The two must be welded together in an unbreakable bond, lest contemporary Christianity become a new religion growing out of man's subjectivism and totally divorced from its roots. What feels good at the moment may have little or nothing to do with the historical Christ. There are all kinds of experiences open to the religious man. Even paganism has its experience content. Actually, a basic characteristic of pagan religion is that it is built on subjective experience rather than historical fact.

This is not a repudiation of religious experience. Christian history shows that the men and women who moved the world for Christ were those who knew Him experientially. One of the strengths of early Methodism was its doctrine of assurance which grew out of an up-to-date experience of the living Christ within one's heart. Far be it from me to downgrade this vital reality which motivates my own life as well as that of millions from every hue and shade of Christendom. What I am insisting is that the Christ whom we love and serve must not be either the historical Jesus who walked in Palestine or the contemporary Lord who is experienced in Chicago. It is not an either-or commitment. It is rather a both-and encounter.

In the previous chapter I sought to make plain my personal choice of Christ above any cause or movement. Care must be taken, however, to point out that the Christ who is priority in my daily living is not some new Jesus of my own taste, but the Jesus who served, died, and was raised from the dead nineteen hundred years ago. This means that I am not free to put words into the mouth of the One chosen as Lord. He cannot become something other than what He is in the pages of the New Testament. It is not valid for me to pick and choose from His life those facets which appeal to me and ignore other aspects of His being. Such a Jesus is not the historical *Christ.* Neither is He my contemporary *Lord.* Only as the Person-priority in my "now" existence is identified as the incarnate Son of God (revealed in the written documents given by those who knew Him in the flesh) can I have a legitimate Christian experience.

It is somewhat disconcerting to some to discover that the New Testament does not major on human experience. Unquestionably the new birth and the coming of the Holy Spirit always are seen in the context of man's inner experience, but the heart of the gospel is far more objective than often is believed. It centers in an event that took place at one precise moment in history. That event can be dated on the calendar. We know where it happened. And it is man's faith in what God did in Jesus Christ who died and rose again that brings salvation from sin and gives purpose to existence. All this is simply a matter of complete trust in a divine, historical act of love. The thin edge of confusion seems to be due to the fact that it is possible to make this leap of faith without a highly-charged emotional experience. And the confusion is doubly confounded by the possibility of being caught up in an exhilarating religious experience without ever honestly making the commitment to the Christ-event necessary for salvation.

Another aspect of the deceptiveness of human experience is seen in the small sharing groups which have sprung up in abundance in the last few years. If they do not degenerate into a mutual exchange of subjective feelings, such groups may be of inestimable value to individual seekers and to the community of faith at large. At times these small groups leave the impression that Jesus is a theme song and a rally cry, but in the actual give-and-take of the meeting, the transforming power is in the human exchange itself. One feels forgiven, transformed, and jubilant because others have loved and understood him. The power of suggestion through group therapy does its work. As long as such a person remains with the supportive group, he is able to keep the fire burning. If he is forced to drop out, or if the group disbands, he discovers that his glowing experience suffers a dim-out. This is probably because his religious experience was dependent on contemporary human relationships rather than on the solidity of the saving work of the historical Christ.

Not all sharing groups are as anemic as that described above. The "house church" is a growing phenomenon in our age, and it is soundly New Testament in its concept. The coming years likely will see more and more of this kind of informal worship and witness. If these groups are to be valid, they will have to find their stability in a careful and systematic study of the Word of God. They will be forced to recognize that witnessing and sharing both within the group and outside its fellowship are strategically important. But they must also keep in mind that in the final analysis salvation is not merely sharing burdens and guilt with one another. Rather, it is an act of personal faith in the redemptive Christ alone.

Personal and group experiences both are subject to deviant direction unless grounded in a sound theology. That is not to impose some strait-laced, sanctimonious, formalized mold around them. It is to relate what I am feeling at this moment to what God did at Calvary long before my day. Furthermore, it is to help shape my existential situation by the sharp Word of Truth which must relate my heart to my mind. Some are now laying claim to radiant experiences of Christ while at the same time living loose sexually, using profane language, and engaging in dishonest relationships. Such an experience may be modern, and it may be religious, but it is not Christian!

Modern man has lived for so long in a sterile vacuum of religious death that he is desperate to find something tangible to which he can cling for assurance. Of course, the sad thing about it is that man must have a crutch for his weak faith. Also, he is in jeopardy in such a situation, since any new thing which comes along can sweep him off his feet if it offers some excitement to replace his dull unfaith. In such a time of religious confusion as that which prevails in our age, men and women turn to the more tangential evidences for religion rather than to Christ Himself. Thus the gifts become so important as to nearly eclipse the Giver. In the exciting manifestation of the Spirit, we all but overlook the cross.

A charismatic revival is sweeping the world. Practically every communion within the Christian world has its share of charismatics. And the phenomenon is also witnessed among people who hold no organized church affiliation. Paul writes at length in 1 Corinthians 12-14 about the spiritual gifts or abilities found in the church at Corinth. A list is given which includes "Apostles, Prophets—those who preach God's Word, Teachers, Those who do miracles, Those who have the gift of healing, Those who can help others, Those who can get others to work together, Those who speak in languages they have never learned" (1 Co 12:28, Living Bible). The list is given in order of the importance of the gifts. Yet, in the charismatic movement it is the last and least of these gifts —that of tongue-speaking—which is given preeminence. Paul does not rule out this gift as being invalid, but he does spend three chapters warning that it may become too important, and it may be misused.

It is not my intention or desire to negate any experience of the Holy Spirit which is meaningful in another person's life. I have no right to do that. It is only in the interest of trying to find the heart of the truth, without which we all are lost, that my observations are made.

One must never declare that speaking in tougues is *the* sign of the baptism or filling of the Holy Spirit. Glossolalia (tongue-speaking) is only one of the gifts, and Paul clearly enunciates the truth that not all Christians are to have the same gifts (1 Co 12:4-11). This provides diversity needed to round out the body of Christ. Christ is the Head of the body, and as far as we know He never spoke in tongues. An added note is needed at this point. Men have been known to speak with strange tongues in pagan rituals, under emotional trauma, and in various forms of dementia without the baptism of the Spirit at all. This obviously means that this gift can be counterfeited. Certainly this does not in any way invalidate the gift of tongues, since only that which is genuine can be counterfeited. But the warning is necessary.

The obsession with glossolalia appears to be an end in itself. People are known to seek this particular gift and to encourage others to do likewise. God's gifts are dispensed by Him to whomever He wills to give them. No man knows what is in the hands of the Lord for any particular individual's ministry. The choice of gifts must be left to God alone, since only He knows what each man is built for. It is interesting to note that nobody seems to be seeking the gifts of prophecy, teaching, miracles, helping, or cooperation—yet, they are all more important in the scale of values than is glossolalia. Occasionally someone seeks the gift of healing, but not often. We seem to be willing to allow God to make the decision in everything except tongue-speaking. It is my opinion that the reason is threefold. Let us look at it.

First, the interest in glossolalia has the marks of child's play. That is not to say that it is bad. Child's play is good, and it is needed by children. Tongues, being the last gift in the list, is on God's lowest shelf. The gift is there so the youngest and weakest Christian may reach it. Some are strong enough that this shelf is bypassed entirely. These people are tall enough to reach a higher gift—helping others, healing the sick, or proclaiming the Word in powerful witness. This does not mean that tongues are unimportant. It only means that for some Christians they are like trying to learn the alphabet when already they are writing beautiful Christian prose. Glossolalia is the gift most sought because most Christians have not advanced beyond this level of faith. Their faith is weak, and they must have something to hold onto in order not to fall. Like an infant learning to walk, they cling to the legs of the table and chairs, a thing more stable and mature persons do not need to do. But only a fool would say, as a result of this, that the supportive table legs are not valid and necessary for the struggling infant.

The claim is made that this gift of tongues is a heavenly language by which the speaker is better able to communicate with God. It should be noted that this is the pattern followed by the infant. Prior to the time when the growing child is able to express himself coherently and intelligibly, he resorts to sounds which, though incomprehensible to others and probably not understood by himself, leaves him with the exhilarating feeling of having communicated in some satisfying manner. As he matures, the inarticulate groanings of infanthood give way to a higher level of communication. As the parent seems to comprehend what the baby is trying to articulate and loves him all the more because of his inadequacy, so God understands the tongues-speaker and lavishes His love upon him. But it is the will of God that every Christian should move beyond this child-stage to the higher shelves.

In his love chapter, the apostle Paul himself suggests that glossolalia is a childish stage in Christian living. He even says that someday all the gifts, including tongues, will disappear. Then comes that famous verse interpreted in many ways through the ages, "When I was a child I spoke and thought and reasoned as a child does. But when I became a man my thoughts grew far beyond those of my childhood, and now I have put away the childish things" (1 Co 13:11, Living Bible). His comparison is specifically directed to the perfection of the world to come, but the relationship to levels of spiritual growth in this life cannot be missed. In fact, Paul's clear admonition is, "Dear brothers, don't be childish in your understanding of these things. Be innocent babies when it comes to planning evil, but be men of intelligence in understanding matters of this kind" (1 Co 14:20, Living Bible). He is telling these beloved Corinthians bluntly to grow up. He says that while he wished all the Corinthians had the gift of speaking in tongues—obviously because they were still such infants in the Lord—he would much prefer that they "were all able to prophesy, preaching God's messages, for that is a greater and more useful power than to speak in unknown languages" (1 Co 14:5, Living Bible). Prophesying is an advanced state of spiritual growth.

Second, the gift of glossolalia is a self-centered experience. That is in keeping with the child's interests referred to above. This is the only gift which is for one's own edification rather than for the church or the world outside. An obsession with the only self-centered gift is risky business, for one of the prime marks of being a Christian is self-denial. Again, Paul states, "A person 'speaking in tongues' helps himself grow spiritually, but one who prophesies, preaching messages from God, helps the entire church grow in holiness and happiness" (1 Co 14:4, Living Bible). No gift was grander in the teaching of Paul than prophesying—that is, preaching the gospel of the cross in a tongue understood by all. This is what he keeps urging the Christians to consider in chapter 14 of 1 Corinthians. As one grows in the grace of Christ, he will be less concerned about what God can do for him (in his disciplined, daily living and witness) and more committed to what he can do for God.

Third, if we are living in the closing days of the age just prior to the coming of the Lord for His church, is it not reasonable to assume that Satan will use every deceptive tactic accessible to him? There is only one way into the kingdom of God, only one way to be ready for the return of Christ. That is by a faith commitment to the saving work of our Lord at Calvary. Speaking in tongues has absolutely nothing to do with it. Having the gift will not give us entrance to the life to come any more than not having it will keep us out. Jesus' concern for the end of the age was not whether men would speak in tongues, but "when the Son of man cometh, shall he find faith on the earth?" (Lk 18:8).

What kind of faith was He talking about? Saving faith! Faith in what God has done for our redemption. Jesus Christ is "the way, the truth, and the life" (Jn 14:6), and no one ever comes to God in any other way.

Satan is an expert in sidetracking good people into something other than the prime essential and getting them hung up in peripheral matters. If he can use a lesser gift of the Spirit (not necessarily by counterfeiting it) to get our eyes off the cross, there is every reason to suspect that he will do it. To become dependent upon a gift rather than the Giver Himself is the surest of all methods used by the devil. To make my relationship with God in any way a matter of possessing certain gifts of the Spirit is to move the center of faith away from the work of Christ. And to do that is to miss the whole thing, to be finally unacceptable to God.

It would be indescribable loss for any man to spend his life sidetracked with the cultivation of spiritual abilities or gifts saying, "Lord, Lord, did we not prophesy in Your name, and in Your name cast out demons, and in Your name perform many miracles?" (Mt 7:22, NASB) only to find that he has bypassed the door to life. To persons like this the Saviour will say, "I never knew you, depart from me." Glossolalia is not mentioned in this list of gifts, but three of the greater gifts are included. I would assume, therefore, that tongue-speaking could suffer the same fate as those abilities enumerated by name. Notice that I said *could*, not *would*, receive severe judgment. Having and employing the gifts of the Holy Spirit does not keep one out of the kingdom unless they become ends in themselves, substitutes for knowing and trusting the historical and experiential Christ.

To condemn the gift of glossolalia (or any other biblical ability named by Paul) would be to grieve the Spirit. But seriously to question an obsession with it is an approach more widely needed. The faithful minister must warn of the grim possibility of being misled in the anxiety over the dispensing of spiritual abilities. The search for tongue-speaking can be frustrating, and the reception of it can produce a combination of spiritual pride and deadly complacency. No one should ever stop at the level of tongues, the lowest shelf. The gift is all right unless it becomes everything. When that happens, it is destructive of one's living relation with the redeeming Christ, as devastating to the true spirit as is a spiritual trip induced by drugs.

In this chapter I have dealt with the Christ of history and the Christ of experience. If He is confined to some remote past, the Lord is dead. But if He is a novel, modern companion detached from His historical person, He is a different Christ altogether. Christ needs to be experienced to be real, but the reality must also be rooted in the historical event. No mystic experience with a subjective Jesus is genuine. I have no dispensation from God to make His Son over into the kind of Jesus that may suit my wishes. Neither is any experience of a divine gift without the ruling priority of the Giver Himself a genuine possession. Therefore, when I declare Christ to be above all, it must be recognized that the Christ of whom I speak is not equated with any of the spiritual abilities, but He is the historical Jesus of the cross known and experienced in the present hour.

Study Questions

1. Many people talk about knowing a Christ who is not at all like the One we meet on the pages of the New Testament. How do you explain this?
2. Can one experience a religious encounter of sharing and love with other people and never discover the efficacy of the saving work of Christ? Explain why this is or is not so.
3. In what way might one confuse "gifts of the Spirit" with a genuine relationship with the Christ of the New Testament?
4. How could glossolalia (speaking in tongues) become a substitute experience for regeneration in Jesus Christ?

4

Faith and Works

AMONG THE OLDEST DEBATES in the Christian religion is the continuing hassle over salvation by faith and salvation by works. It would seem that there should be no problem here in view of Paul's summary statement, "By grace are ye saved through faith. . . . Not of works, lest any man should boast" (Eph 2:8-9). That would appear to be clear enough. But then James adds a note which clouds the issue for some, "Faith without works is dead" (Ja 2:20). Who is right? One of the cardinal doctrines of the Protestant Reformation was salvation by faith *alone*. The emphasis was needed to correct what was believed to be a lopsided stress on the efficacy of works in the old Roman church. Since the days of Luther, efforts have been made by some to restore works to a more respectable place as a form of counterbalance.

Not much theological bitterness exists today over this doctrinal issue except in the ultraextreme groups at either end of the theological spectrum. But in actual day-to-day practical living among persons related to the Christian enterprise, the dichotomy is clearly discerned. In the more pronounced instances there are those who see no need to do anything because they believe. Faith is a cure-all beyond which there can be nothing else. Even to hint that what a man does is of eternal worth is to cast an unhappy reflection on the exclusive power of faith. Persons of the opposing view often argue that God will not do for man what he can do for himself. In this light every good work is of vital significance to man's relationship with God, and it is presumptuous to put all the responsibility on the Lord. Between these two opposites are found diverse shades of one or the other position.

We who choose to be called evangelicals are almost unanimously agreed that man both obtains and retains his salvation by faith only—not by works. Inconsistencies occasionally crop up which cannot be justified by any amount of rationalization, no matter how we seek to explain them. I have in mind the declared necessity of water baptism, the mystic power of infant baptism, and the avowed change brought about by confirmation. In every case, however, the individual or doctrinal group will argue for the primacy of faith as the means of salvation.

Because of the exclusive emphasis which evangelicals give to faith (sometimes diluted by ritualistic acts which provide sensory evidence), we are accused of being hearers without being doers of the Word. We are said to be pietistic—implying that we withdraw into a smug little cocoon of personal salvation unrelated to the world around us—rather than socialistic. To be saved by faith alone is assumed by many to be the same thing as to be selfishly isolated. Their logic comes from what they see or do not see in our lives. After we commit ourselves in faith, far too many of us sit down as though we were determined not to give God any help. In fact, it looks almost as though some of us are afraid to engage in works of righteousness for fear that someone will think that we doubt or distrust the full sufficiency of our faith!

Ordinarily, when men and women desire to be religious but reject salvation by faith alone, they become actively involved in as much charitable social work as is humanly possible. If these welfare programs are attached in some way to the church, the satisfaction received is greatly increased. All types of worthy federal and community programs for the alleviation of human suffering and need have developed out of a natural humanitarian concern and a desire to make a contribution to our world. What could be more religious than that? And with this rationale, the church rightly becomes a part of the action, and men and women decide that they are literally working out their salvation—actually earning a right to the kingdom!

The subtle thing about it is that one can be a follower of Christ's way without being a participant in Christ's death. To act like Jesus is not foreign to the disciplined life. But let us not miss the fact that we are still only *imitations* of the Lord. Imitations have their place in both secular and sacred realms of operation, but they are not the real thing. This is why Paul keeps talking about being "in Christ." Man must cease being an imitation and become a real part of Christ's body, a partaker of His nature, a sharer in His death and resurrection. And clearly this is not done by any kind of works. It is wholly a matter of faith. Thus the humanitarian concern which opens our hands and our hearts to a neighbor in need is a Christian duty, but it is not the source of the Christian's life in God.

A good Buddhist is one who follows the path that Buddha traveled. He imitates his religious mentor. The same thing can be said about the Muslim. Every religion known to man, except Christianity, is a do-it-yourself way of life. Man earns his salvation by what he does. In Christianity no one earns salvation. My hope rests not on what I can *do*, but on what He has *done*. That is the basic distinction between Christianity and all other religions. Perhaps that is why I have an aversion to referring to my faith as religion. It is so completely distinctive that the word just does not appropriately fit it.

What, then, is the place of works in the Christian life?

First, let it be emphatically stated that works belong in every believer's list of priorities. A sizeable amount of works should attend every valid faith commitment. James insists that faith is proved by works. "You say the way to God is by faith alone, plus nothing; well, I say that good works are important too, for without good works you can't prove whether you have faith or not; but anyone can see that I have faith by the way I act" (Ja 2:18, Living Bible). Anyone who does nothing about his faith will find it difficult to convince others that he has faith at all. The result will be that his witness falls on deaf ears. On the other hand, the person who does all sorts of good works without possessing a saving faith may deceive himself and others, but he will not impress God. Faith or works alone is a dead thing. Like love and marriage, they belong together. Love should issue in marriage, and marriage should indicate to others that love is present. The fly in the ointment is that while love develops into marriage, marriage is no guarantee of love. The analogy is obvious.

If only I could get all the wonderful, hardworking people in my church to trust in Christ's atoning work rather than their own deeds, what a glorious change would come into their lives! Likewise, if I could encourage those persons who have made a commitment to Christ in faith to become fully engaged in the work of the ministry rather than resting on their one act of trust, what a change there would be in the effectiveness of the local parish. Outsiders notice the power and influence of the Christian only when he refuses to be either a faith disciple or a works enthusiast. He must be both.

But is there a priority to be given to one or the other of these two aspects of discipleship? Man never arrives at the divine purpose for his existence by working *toward* the cross. Another way of saying this is that works prior to faith may do no harm, but neither do they effect the good which the Creator has designed for us. Salvation begins at Calvary—

nowhere else. And until it begins, it cannot grow. Therefore, instead of working *toward* the cross, the Christian works *from* it. He does not worship because he serves, but he serves because he worships. Worship and service must dwell together. Nevertheless, worship must precede service if it is to be genuinely Christian.

It is my duty to serve God. But it is far more than a duty—it is my coveted privilege. My prime reason for working in the vineyard of the world is not because there is within me a stalwart obedience to my duty. Rather it is because I love the Lord. It is this quality of love toward Him who has redeemed me that motivates my work. Never is there a thought of laying claim to what God owes me for labor rendered, but only the thought of rendering service because of what I owe to God. My own faith commitment has thrust me into a life of Christian ministry, not vice versa. In this sense, faith has priority over works.

No one worked harder in the religious realm than did a young man who studied at the feet of Gamaliel. In a frenzied determination to work himself into favor with God, Saul of Tarsus dedicated himself to a rigorous and disciplined pursual of service to his Jewish faith. Then one noonday he met the Lord, and he saw his selfrighteous labors in their true light. He recognized them as unavailing human efforts which brought no sense of certainty that God had accepted him. But when Saul made a commitment of his life to Christ in faith (a commitment to which he referred constantly in his letters), he made a new beginning. His works increased, but his motivation had changed. Now he worked *from* the cross. His whole attitude was altered so that henceforth he took pride in nothing which he himself did. His only pride was in the finished work of the cross of Christ which took priority over any and all good works he performed.

The law of Moses was a "schoolmaster to bring us unto

Christ" (Gal. 3:24). That is, the Mosaic law was not an end in itself. It pointed to a God-man relationship which could only be realized by perfect obedience. Thus the law was a means to an end—the end being the establishment of a "kingdom of priests, and an holy nation" (Ex 19:6, see Deu 7:6). The nation of Israel would become the kingdom of God to the degree in which its elected citizenry obeyed the divine mandate as given in the Ten Commandments. Significantly, an annual Day of Atonement was observed because no man was successful in keeping the whole law. Man's acceptance rested ultimately upon God's grace, not upon human fulfillment of the divine command.

Many archetypes of New Testament truth are found in the Old Testament. Among them is the Day of Atonement, which pointed to that bleak but blessed Friday when God would atone for the sins of the world in the death of His own Son. Henceforth, as Paul put it, "we are no longer under a schoolmaster. For ye are all the children of God by faith in Christ Jesus" (Gal 3:25-26). The law of Moses, therefore, was given to man to reveal his inability to measure up to the divine requirement for membership in the kingdom. Ultimately man would be driven to the cross, where by faith in God's substitutionary work he would find his estrangement annulled and his reconciliation effected. This is the meaning of the apostle's words, "A man is not justified by the works of the law, but by the faith of Jesus Christ, . . . for by the works of the law shall no flesh be justified" (Gal 2:16).

The Christian should understand this. But still there are numberless hosts of church people who believe that they will be saved by their good works. Such persons usually refer to the Sermon on the Mount (Mt 5-7) as the code of ethics by which they try to live. It is their questionable hope that they may be able to obey well enough to gain admittance into the kingdom of heaven. If I thought for one moment that my chances of entering the kingdom were dependent upon my living up to the Sermon on the Mount, I would die of fright! This is why I cannot understand the reductionist who insists that all one has to do to be a Christian is to apply the principles laid down in that sermon to the living of his life.

Actually, the Sermon on the Mount is an intensification of the Ten Commandments. And if no one has ever been successful in living up to the Mosaic law, how can he expect to keep the more severe Messianic requirement? In a real sense, Christ is presented by Matthew as the new Moses, head of a new humanity in a community of faith. The law is not rescinded at any point. In fact, Jesus was specific when He said, "Till heaven and earth pass, one jot or one tittle shall in no wise pass from the law, till all be fulfilled" (Mt 5:18). Christ went far beyond the Decalogue in demanding a righteousness which *exceeds* that of the Pharisees (Mt 5:20) who spent their lives in a desperate attempt to keep the law. He even had the audacity to say, "Be ye therefore perfect, even as your Father which is in heaven is perfect" (Mt 5:48). And the perfection of which He spoke is not moral or ethical perfection at all. That would be hard enough. Rather it is the complete actualization of that design and purpose intended for us by God from creation. Who on earth has ever achieved that by his works?

Nothing short of perfection is acceptable with God. Thus we are under divine judgment due to our miserable failure to achieve. If the Ten Commandments revealed the futility of man's works for admission into the kingdom, how much more does the Sermon on the Mount conclusively expose the deficiency in our works of righteousness! This sermon, far from making the Christian life simple, lays down basic characteristics which are well-nigh impossible. Yet, this is no ethic for the millenial age. It is God's requirement of us right now. No wonder these intensive commands terrify me.

The chasm is so wide between what is prescribed and what I actually do that all my works stand condemned.

Let us remember that the Sermon on the Mount is not a code of ethics such as is found in nonchristian religions. We do not become righteous or obtain salvation by keeping laws. These characteristics do not *make* us Christian by our obedience. On the contrary, they insist that men are to live like this because they *are* Christians. And that is where the rub comes. Not even the best of Christians qualifies for acceptance on the basis of these Christlike characteristics.

What, then, is the meaning of the Sermon on the Mount? Once man is brought to Christ, by the exposure of his "falling short of the glory of God," as witnessed to by the awesome commands of the Old Testament, he is immediately made to see that there is no way to satisfy Christ by works (as there was no way to satisfy God by the Jew's keeping of the law) either before or after conversion. Having accepted the grace of God by faith in Jesus Christ, every Christian must live out all his days under the intensified expectation of a new humanity. Neither before nor after the cross is any man saved by his works. More is expected of the Christian than of the nonbeliever—and he will do more if he is genuinely converted—but he can never earn his place with God. Our failure to equate our living with the characteristics of a disciple as seen in the Sermon on the Mount continues again and again to throw us back on the mercy of God for our salvation. And it is at this point where we must see the priority of faith over works.

Works are an essential part of man's salvation experience in its progressive unfolding. We may rightly doubt a man's dedication to the serving Christ if he does nothing for his Lord. Notwithstanding, it is my considered judgment that these works must be a byproduct of faith if they are to be legitimate. When works become a substitute for faith, they assume a preeminence which they were never meant to have.

Man's work must never be granted precedence over the work of Christ. His work on the cross precedes and overshadows our works of righteousness. And our faith must be solidly anchored to His saving work rather than our own.

First and foremost, then, "I know whom I have believed, and am persuaded that He is able to keep that which I have committed unto him against that day" (2 Ti 1:12). With this assurance springing out of my declared priority of faith, I will

> Work, for the night is coming,
> Work thro' the morning hours;
> Work while the dew is sparkling;
> Work, 'mid springing flowers.
> Work when the day grows brighter,
> Work in the glowing sun;
> Work, for the night is coming,
> When man's work is done.
>
> ANNA L. COGHILL

STUDY QUESTIONS

1. What specifically was Luther reacting against when he insisted on salvation by faith only?
2. Explain the basic distinction between Christianity and the world religions. What do we mean by do-it-yourself religion?
3. What is the role of works in the life of a Christian?
4. Discuss the fundamental flaw in working *toward* the cross as contrasted with working *from* the cross.

5

Truth and Tradition

When the churchmen from the Jewish center in Jerusalem questioned Jesus as to why He allowed the twelve to eat with uncleansed hands, thus transgressing the tradition of the elders, He countered with a question of His own: "Why do ye also transgress the commandment of God by your tradition?" (Mt 15:3, see Mk 7:1-23). Then followed one of the Master's illuminating illustrations which had to do with the customary treatment of aging parents in contradiction of the fifth commandment. He could have presented as evidence numerous other examples of their confusing preference for human tradition to divine truth, but this one specimen was adequate. Though the disciples expressed their concern about the offense taken by the churchmen, there is no recorded vocal exchange by which the Jewish traditionalists defended their questionable custom. Perhaps inwardly they acknowledged their own indefensible position.

In his letters to the Galatians and the Colossians, the apostle Paul cautions against "the traditions of my fathers" and "human tradition." But in the second epistle to Thessalonica he speaks with high regard of tradition. "Stand fast, and hold the traditions which ye have been taught, whether by word, or our epistle" (2 Th 2:15). *The Living Bible* takes the liberty allowed in paraphrasing to render this exhortation, "Stand firm and keep a strong grip on *the truth* that we taught you" (italics added). There is no doubt that this is the thought in Paul's mind. And the criterion by which the apostle determines the truth of God (passed through human mediums like the biblical writers) and the tradition of man is made clear in an earlier reference where the life, teaching, and work of Christ is the finalizing factor (Col 2:8). Galatians 1:14 speaks of Paul's actions prior to his conversion based on the traditions of the Jewish elders in contrast with his base of authority following that climactic event.

A note of clarification is needed here lest one conjecture that the Pauline concept of truth excludes the Old Testament Scriptures. Although he was a proponent of grace rather than law, Paul never would have agreed to any understanding of the Old Testament as being only the traditions of men. It was he who instructed young Timothy that "All scripture is given by inspiration of God" (2 Ti 3:16). And the Scripture to which he made reference was that within the Hebrew canon—our Old Testament. None had appeared in the form of the New Testament as yet.

When the early church drew up the canon of the Christian Scriptures, they were careful to reject everything which smacked of human tradition void of the divine Word. The core of truth handed down from the apostles and disciples who knew Christ in the flesh was the measuring rod by which our twenty-seven separate writings were included and others rejected. Since continuing archeological finds and textual examination tend only to confirm the integrity of the Bible, it is apparent that the guidelines used by both the Jewish and Christian communities were established by the Holy Spirit.

Most of our ambiguity in the modern church is caused by a rejection of the biblical content as divine truth. Determined moves are being made to rediscover what scholarship calls "the historical Jesus." I have used this expression in this book to describe the Christ who lived in Palestine at the beginning of the Christian era. This is what the scholars imply by the words, but often it is insisted that one does not get back to the historical Jesus without peeling away the traditions about Him which are preserved in the biblical narratives. This means that much of the gospel record is not to be trusted. It must be "demythologized"—a much overworked term meaning to rid Jesus of the supernatural aura that surrounds Him in the Bible—if the real Jesus is to be discovered. Persons who share this irreverent concept of the Scriptures assume them to be filled with human traditions and not always consistent with divine truth except in some strained, germ-of-general-truth manner.

My own line of demarcation is not at some fuzzy divide of my own choosing within the biblical revelation. On the contrary, it is at the point of Scripture versus nonscripture or extrascripture. The Bible is a closed book inosfar as it is divine revelation given to the world through chosen human mediums supervised by the Holy Spirit. There is nothing mechanical about such a view, but there is something very definite about it. Nothing can be added to or deleted from the biblical writings. Where the Scripture speaks (except in those instances where the writer explains that he is giving his opinion with no word from the Lord), I find my priority. The Word of God within the written revelation is truth. Everything else, good and needful as I may believe it to be, is "the tradition of the elders" or purely human judgment.

Shortly before His crucifixion, when Jesus knew that the hour was growing late, He prayed for His disciples that they might be consecrated by the Father to continue His divine work. His burden was that they be sanctified in the truth. And no uncertainty is permitted in the Lord's definition of that truth. Terse enough to strike an indelible impression, His words were, "Thy word is truth" (Jn 17:17). Debate has run round and round that statement by men who cannot make up their minds what "word" Jesus was talking about. That He was thinking of the written word given by God to His chosen servants who penned the Hebrew Scriptures would appear to be unmistakable. Jesus had a high regard for Scripture.

People always are asking how one can know that the Bible is true. There is within every man the unavoidable need to drive his stakes down somewhere. Every new discovery of late proves the truth of something in the Bible which was long doubted.

Whether one believes the Bible to be truth ultimately will depend on what he thinks about Jesus Christ. If Christ is for him the divine Son of God, then the Scriptures which declare Him will be accepted as truth. If Jesus is only a good man, there will be real reservations about the Bible's authority. And if one does not choose Christ and the written Word about Him, he will inevitably select some other standard of truth as his personal priority. Therefore, it becomes a matter of deciding whether it is to be the truth of God as recorded in the Scriptures, or the traditions of men as freely and widely circulated in our eclectic age. One simply has to make a choice and stick with it. And that choice is directly related and finally decided by man's opinion of Jesus Christ.

Traditions are as plentiful as dandelions. And they are just as colorful and just as hard to get rid of. Every Christian group from the mammoth Roman Catholic church to the tiny, independent local congregation has its own man-made dogma which sets it apart. And within both the mammoth communion and the autonomous parish are to be uncovered interesting varieties of cherished traditions handed down from parent to child. At some times it is a form of folk religion, while at other times it is no more than a clannish or family indoctrination. Even within the family, the smallest social and religious unit, there seldom are as many as two persons who hold precisely the same detailed dogma. Each man has his own private traditions.

For me, the contents of the Bible do not fall into the category of tradition, even though the term *traditional* is used to define religious views whose roots are in apostolic times. Traditional often means an older style in contrast to contemporary—traditional and contemporary furniture, for example. But a traditional religion may be as new as tomorrow morning if it is created from some current human tradition. In the same way, some very contemporary religious concepts may be very old and also very true since there is something quite timeless about truth. The biblical message, therefore, does not fit the image of tradition (cherished human concepts). Conversely, it speaks to me of valid and eternal contemporaneity (ultimate and changeless truth).

If Christ is authoritative for me, then the biblical content is also binding. The Master referred to and quoted from the Old Testament. He even believed the story of Noah and the flood (Mt 24:37-39) as well as Jonah and the fish (Mt 12:38-41). True, He did draw some new conclusions from the law in His Sermon on the Mount (Mt 5:17-48) but in each instance He amplified the command. In no case did the Son of God take issue with the written Word except to bring out its more legitimate meaning which had been missed by the legalistic religionists. He cleared up any hazy misgivings about His attitude to the law when He said, "Not the smallest letter or stroke shall pass away from the Law, until all is accomplished." (Mt 5:18, NASB). Never do we find Jesus explaining away any biblical passage by making it into a myth or doubting its authenticity. Surely, He must be my pattern here. I cannot hold the Scriptures lightly when Christ held them in such an exalted position—that is, if He really is my Lord and honestly does come first in my life.

The traditions of the elders, to which both Jesus and Paul

had something to say, were a multiplicity of manmade restrictions and pronouncements developing out of the Decalogue. Serving God on the basis of the scribal tradition was a burdensome task which only the professional Pharisees had either the time or the disposition to perform. For the common laboring people of the land, there was little chance of being accepted by God. The kingdom of God was reserved for "the separated ones" who had the good fortune to make an occupation out of keeping the maze of meticulous legalities.

There were times when a fanatical adherence to these scribal laws made it unlikely, if not impossible, to keep the divine law as given to Moses at the beginning of Hebrew national life. This is what Jesus was attacking when He deliberately drew attention to the desecration of the Sabbath day by obedience to human traditions. These only frustrated man's efforts to serve God and defeated the Creator's purpose to serve man.

Being a part of Protestantism means that certain specified beliefs and attitudes should grace my existence. Being a member of a specific denomination involves additional traditions. My being a clergyman puts another spice into the mixture. And to top it all off, I am an evangelical, and such people are supposed to hold different views. Thus I find that my lifestyle and form of ministry are boxed in by an abundance of traditions which have a way of becoming sacrosanct without my knowing that such a thing has happened or why. It is usually at the point of nonbiblical traditions that one is apt to become overweening in his arrogant vanity.

A resolve to rid myself of traditional strictures is a must. Let me say again that this has nothing necessarily to do with ancient beliefs. It has to do with the opinions of men (whether of those who lived long ago or of those who are alive at this moment) which can speak to me in the place of God.

Only as my mind is freed from nonbiblical voices can I be free enough to hear and respond to the Word of the Lord within the revealed and written truth. Man may be listened to and his opinions courteously considered, but nothing he says can be accepted if it contradicts the revelation of Scripture as recorded by inspired writers and sanctioned by Christ Himself. There is a real place for reason, but it can never be allowed to take the place of revelation. Reason may well illuminate revelation, but revelation purifies reason!

Human tradition can become a source of great pride on the part of persons who, like the Pharisees, take satisfaction in living up to some human standard. At the same time, such tradition can induce nothing short of mental malaise for persons who feel the pressure to conform to be a weight heavier than they can support. Being by nature religious animals, these people have to do one of three things. They may live under the burden of tradition with an intolerable guilt, or they may discard tradition altogether with an admission that religion itself is not for them. A third and better response to such an unsettling situation is to take a careful look at what is held to be divine truth, and prayerfully, on the basis of scriptural revelation alone, sort the commandments of God from the traditions of men.

A case in point is a sacrosanct attitude toward the proper pattern of public worship. Since my childhood, I have suffered feelings of guilt at the thought of any design for public worship that did not include Sunday morning, Sunday evening, and Wednesday night. For many years my pastoral ministry was stultified by the idea that eleven o'clock Sunday morning is a time for formal praise, the evening service is an hour for evangelism, and the midweek period is an informal time for devotional study and fellowship. Although there is nothing wrong with this plan, it must be admitted that the Bible nowhere demands such a rigid divisional design.

Who says a church must have Sunday evening service and

that it must be evangelistic? Maybe more people would come to church in the morning if it were more evangelistically oriented and provided the only chance for public worship that day. And who says another service has to be conducted on Wednesday night? What about Tuesday or Thursday? And Sunday school? Would it be better to have it Sunday evening or at several different times during the week for persons who cannot fit an inflexible time mold? And why shouldn't some of these class sessions be held in homes rather than the church building? The reason we get so uptight about such innovative ideas is not because of dedication to truth but because of bondage to tradition.

Another illustration of putting human tradition before divine truth is the almost universal insistence among church people that some kind of double standard exists for the moral life of men and women. Our day has seen more of a breaking down of this wall than ever before. The trouble with the changing climate, however, is that it has not bettered the situation; it has only made it worse. Instead of making adultery and marital unfaithfulness as bad for a man as for a woman, the trend is to make it no worse for a woman than for a man. The difference may seem negligible on the surface, but it is much deeper than it appears. There is a terrible difference. While the double standard should have been discarded in order to lift the moral sensitivity of the man, what it has actually done is to reduce the sensitivity of the woman. Nowhere does the Bible sanction a double standard of morals. Sin is as bad for one sex as for the other. Neither does the Scripture endorse lowering the standard to effect equality. Divine truth says that immorality and infidelity are wrong, and "God is no respecter of persons" (Ac 10:34). Human tradition which annuls any part of that truth is a contributing factor in our world of confused values and moral degeneration.

Some of us hold such inflexible, condemnatory attitudes

toward the use of alcoholic beverages that we cannot have fellowship with an evangelical Christian who tastes strong drink. We would have been ill at ease around Martin Luther, to whom beer was a part of daily life. In fact, while we might have had something in common with John the Baptist, we would have been disappointed with Christ at this point. Listen to Jesus' own words: "John the Baptist used to go without food and never took a drop of liquor all his life, . . . But I eat my food and drink my wine." (Lk 7:33-34, Living Bible). I will be among the first to do battle against the exploitation of the public on the part of manufacturers and sellers of alcoholic beverages. I have seen what this traffic can do to a man. But my reasons are rooted in the destruction and despair resultant from excessive use of intoxicants, not from any strict biblical prohibition. Nowhere does the Bible forbid the use of strong drink, though it is consistent in its demands for temperance. Let us at least be honest in our stance. Abstinance is a good tradition, but let us not try to make it better by misusing the Word of God to support it.

It is not my intention to disqualify all tradition. There are many excellent traditions which house eternal truths. I have tried to say only two things in reference to the place of the tradition of the elders. First, every man must distinguish carefully between divine truth and human concepts. Second, having made the distinction, he must choose truth over tradition wherever it is obvious that a conflict is present. My mandate for living is the Word of God, not the word of man.

Study Questions

1. How would you define the "core of truth" as handed down by the writers of the Scripture?
2. In what way is one's view of Scripture directly related to his view of Jesus Christ?

3. Think of some sacrosanct traditions held tenaciously by your own church. Are they valid? Does the Scripture reinforce them? Are they elevated above the biblical revelation? Do they tend to separate people unnecessarily?
4. How could the church advocate the support of its nonbiblical traditions which are ethically good, while at the same time honestly admitting that they are not a part of the explicit commandment of God?

6

Salvation or Liberation?

FOR ALMOST TWENTY CENTURIES, the Christian church has been dedicated to the proclamation of the Word of salvation. On many side issues, the splintering groups could not agree. Nevertheless, if an honest poll had been taken, generally it would have been agreed that the church has one distinct mission in the world. God had placed His church in the midst of a fallen race to bring the good news of salvation to all. Her task is to tell of God's act of redemption in Jesus Christ, by whom "whosoever believeth . . . should not perish, but have everlasting life" (Jn 3:16).

If Timothy had had any questions about the meaning of what had happened on the cross, none remained after he received his first letter from Paul. There he read the words, "How true it is, and how I long that everyone should know it, that Christ Jesus came into the world to save sinners" (1 Ti 1:15, Living Bible). For the first nineteen hundred years of its existence, the church has shared that passion and priority.

Salvation means something very special. Isaiah foresaw the birth of a son whom he called Emmanuel (God with us), born of a virgin (Is 7:14). Joseph was later informed that the child in Mary's womb was that promised Son who would "save his people from their sins" (Mt 1:21). The Samaritans, who were introduced to Jesus by the woman at the well, discovered what the church was destined to preach: "We know that this is indeed the Christ, the Saviour of the world" (Jn 4:42). For them, salvation was a very personal matter which began with the conversion of the individual. After that, it spread like wildfire into society, where wrongs were righted among men, and even kings were challenged in their evil rule. But it always began with one man or one woman. God does not count noses the way man does, creating a depersonalized world. The Father in heaven sees only one. Every person is a *one*—one unique individual for whom Christ died. And that one man, sinner though he is, can appropriate divine forgiveness for himself by faith in Christ's sacrificial work on the cross. That was the heart of the church's teaching, preaching, and service until modern times.

In our day, the word "saved" has become a bit old fashioned sounding. Sophisticated man acts as though he does not know what the word means. It no longer communicates. All such salvation words must be junked, and new terms must replace them. A reference to God's *saving* men may embarrass some individuals. Only the more fundamentalistic fellowships still use the term with the honor and respect it deserves.

In actuality, our problem is not one of words so much as it is one of concepts. The matter of semantics needs to be considered in any communicative procedure, but too often our distorted concept of the mission of the church is blamed on a semantic difficulty. We need to come clean with each other within the church. And the church needs to come clean with the world.

Never before have there been so many highly educated and professionally trained religious leaders who fail to say anything which the general public can understand. The reason for this is that we are trying to talk out of both sides of our mouths while laying blame for the source of confusion at the feet of semantic scrapegoats.

Deep inside many church leaders is a sense of frustration and guilt left by a failure to get on with the mission of the church. That mission is hard work, and the path of least resistance is always enticing. So many good things need to be done in so many areas that Christians often discover themselves being diverted from the main highway into less strenuous and more acceptable sidepaths of endeavor. And to salve our consciences, we adopt religious names for all our committees and agencies. As a Christian, one must be engaged in Christian work, but how easy it is to tack a Christian title on whatever we decide to do. And how very hard it is to *do* what the New Testament defines as Christian. It is more than semantics. The whole problem rises out of concepts.

The new concept of the church's mission is defined by the term liberation, rather than by the older word salvation. Although it is usually argued that the new definitive title for the Christian church's work in the world is more inclusive and embraces within it the idea of salvation, the argument fails to convince many people. What I see in the new liberation concept—regardless of what its proponents claim the word means—is a form of mission without salvation. Pervading the worldwide community called by Christ's name is a new version of the mission of Christianity. One might call it a revised version, but it is not so much revision as it is replacement. In that sense, it is *new*, a result of the new theology and the new ethic about which all of us have heard so much.

In the liberation theology there is little if any salvation history. Everything is relative to the current world situation and has little to do with any kind of ultimate dependence on what happened on the cross of Calvary. God is in the process, and both the past and the future seem unimportant in comparison to the present. The goal is the best kind of social and political existence for each man in this world.

At times it appears as if the present world is all there ever can be. Since this is so, each person must get all he can at once.

Liberation theology sees the church as a means of involvement with this sociopolitical revolution. It seeks to help all people who are struggling for immediate liberation from whatever cramps or halters them. When this objective is achieved, the Christian community will have accomplished its mission—not salvation, but liberation. In this manner, man will have accomplished what he set out to do at the Tower of Babel—to build the kingdom of God. But his god will be a human concept rather than a divine entity.

Although it must be included in the church's engagement with the world, human liberation can be equated in no sense with divine salvation. God is concerned with man's earthly betterment and political and social emancipation, but He is more interested in man's eternal well-being. What God wants for His people is spiritual stability which will remain when all earthly support fails. It is the genius of the divine mind that it offers something solid when humanizing efforts and humanitarian objectives collapse. Man needs something to depend upon when he no longer can trust the rungs of a worn out ladder raised by well-meaning people bent on climbing to some liberated utopia.

There is a place for civil disobedience and even revolution, but this is the exception, never the rule. Our generation has seen this "last resort technique" being used once a day and twice on Sundays. *The world is in ferment, and anarchy has become fashionable.* Christians are being told that every man and every nation must be free, for nothing else is in keeping with the ethic of the church. Therefore, Christians feel they must support revolution. And not infrequently, councils of churchmen go on record endorsing every new uprising as though they speak for the entire constituency of the Christian world. In reality, of course, they speak only for themselves.

Out of the widespread environment of revolutionary attempts by small countries has grown the excessive obsession for liberation of all kinds. Citizens demand freedom from the oppression of law and order; young people cry for liberation from parental authority; students declare themselves unwilling to live under any semblance of institutional administration in which they do not have an upper hand. No end is in sight for the victimization of masses of people in the struggle for freedom from discrimination toward minority groups. Draftees burn their draft cards in defiance of the military system and evade their responsibilities by fleeing across the border into neighboring countries. Women's Liberation has now joined the ranks of groups with an intent to have their message heard. And finally, the gay folk are demanding freedom from stigma and recognition of their deviant moral lifestyle as only one of several normal approaches to sexual fulfillment. In each of these instances, the church has been deeply involved as though this were the only mission given it.

Through these overzealous matters of liberation, plus others far too numerous to include here, churches and individuals focus their pent-up energies and emotional empathies into safe diversions. In this way one's gaze can be kept concentrated on absorbing issues which spare him from looking honestly at his own heart. Scriptural truth has become so distorted by our philosophical relativism that the general concensus is to accept the concept of sociopolitical liberation in lieu of that of biblical salvation. What is even worse is the possibility that it is not a choice between liberation and salvation, but an inability to tell the difference.

It must be pointed out at this point that social, economic, and political liberation are not contrary to the ethic of either the Old or the New Testament. Such freedom is part and parcel of Jesus' mission in the world. When our Lord stood to read the Scripture in His hometown synagogue, He chose words from Isaiah: "The Spirit of the Lord is upon me, because he hath anointed me to preach the gospel to the poor; he hath sent me to heal the brokenhearted, to preach *deliverance to the captives,* and recovering of sight to the blind, to *set at liberty* them that are bruised, To preach the acceptable year of the Lord" (Lk 4:18-19, italics added). Indeed, Jesus described His mission as Messianic. Only He can finally bring about such liberation. But we are a part of His body and, therefore, privileged and destined to share in His work of liberating all peoples.

What I am saying is not that liberation is wrong, but that it is inadequate. Social, economic, and political liberation cannot be accepted as *the* gospel. Such betterment of earthly existence must stand on its own feet and not pretend to negate the need for eternal salvation from sin and death. To devote *all* energies to such liberation is to fail at the point of the church's greatest challenge. The priority of the Christian church is to lead man into a new life of salvation from his debilitating and damning sin. Without that, there is nothing of lasting value in any of mankind's liberations.

Christians, of all people, should know that all men have to live under some kind of civil, social, and religious control. Even if we did not know this by pure logic and reason alone, we could not miss the classic way in which the Hebrew Scriptures make this truth plain. Adam was quite modern. He wanted to be free. In spite of all he had, there was one thing he did not possess, and he was dead set on having it. Adam was convinced that a man could not be happy or fully human as long as he did not possess total freedom in every facet of his earthly life. So he demanded liberation. And he got it. But in the bargain, he lost salvation. Such a fate should never come to any man. Nonetheless, it has happened to every generation since the first.

The making of a man is an inside job. If he cannot find it on the inside, he will never find it anywhere else. What man needs most is not a liberation dependent upon circumstances under which he has to live. Nothing short of perfection in this liberated state will satisfy the modern Adam within us in its demands for autonomous freedom. Manifest to all of us is the fact that perfection is impossible. And without the full and complete realization of his demand for sociopolitical freedom, man remains discontent. Feeling that he is unjustly treated, his search for anarchistic freedom continues because he knows that still he is not liberated.

Liberation is an evasive thing. So slippery is it that one's hands never seem to grasp it. Just when it looks as if it is within reach and man reaches out his fingers to touch it, the whole dream bursts like a soap bubble. Salvation is so different. It does not elude us at all. Any man can have it in utter fullness if he wills. Nothing about it ever disappoints us. That is because it does not depend upon circumstances being perfect or even good. What it is dependent upon is relationship. And that is an inner, not an outward thing. This is why I say that the making of a man is an inside job. In light of this observation, the words of Jesus take on new meaning: "If therefore the Son shall make you free, you shall be free indeed" (Jn 8:36, NASB). Real freedom is not human liberation but divine salvation.

It may be said that the basic contrast between these two forms of freedom is seen in their inherent natures. Liberation reflects the idea of being free from other persons or outside restraints placed upon me by society. Salvation suggests the concept of being free from my own uncontrollable self and the undesirable mastery which it holds over me. Regardless of the degree of liberation I may achieve, I am still in need of salvation. Frankly, the more liberated I am, the more definitely do I stand in need of salvation from self. Unless there is a new Master within to save me from my obsession with selfish ambitions, my liberation will become intolerably dangerous. On the other hand, when salvation comes to my heart and mind (an inner consciousness of acceptance with God through Christ), I am thereby instantly liberated.

What I have insisted on here is that, while certain forms of liberation are an integral facet of the Messianic mission in the world, priority must be given to salvation. Liberation is not a substitute, not a replacement. It is not even a revision. A better word would be *supplement*, but even then the supplementary civil, social, and religious freedom must be controlled by some form of disciplinary guidelines determined by the nature of salvation.

Study Questions

1. What do you consider to be the basic task of the church in today's world? Support your answer. At what biblical points do you find clear expression of your conviction?
2. Define the word *salvation.* Does it differ from the contemporary idea of *liberation?* If so, in what manner is this to be explained?
3. How deeply engaged with good humanitarian objectives should the Christian church become? Is it possible for these ends to be substituted for more legitimate priorities?
4. When is a man really free? Is freedom an inner or outer condition? Is there a relationship between the two?

7

Uniformity or Diversity?

POLARIZATION has become an ugly word in the religious world. The mere mention of it strikes fear into the hearts of people who are wed to the establishment. The last thing any Christian should do is to hint that division within an ecclesiastical organization might have some merit. That is, it is the last thing one should be guilty of doing if he values the respect and comraderie of his peers. My own reputation has not been enhanced by any of the numerous occasions when it has been my honest opinion that I should speak out against serious trends toward secular humanism within the institutional church. Members of my local parish do not always appreciate what must appear at times to be undue criticism. The irony is that the statements may be nothing more than the giving of a factual report which throws a bad light on the institution. If these facts are made public, the reporter is immediately accused of being critical and attempting to split the church.

The respectable thing for a Christian today is to acquiesce to whatever the highest voices in the ascending power structure have to say. These persons either have been duly elected or properly appointed; therefore, it is assumed that they become practically infallible. When they speak ex cathedra, we are all supposed to get in line. In the final analysis, most Protestant groups have their infallible papal power. It may or may not be one leading voice; it may be a small aggregate of voices who speak as one. We fool ourselves if we smile at the Catholic idea of the infallibility of the pope and congratulate ourselves on having no such pompous, pontifical cadre.

Some of us have as much trouble bowing to this pontificate as did Luther and Wesley. Conformity at the expense of conviction is too great a price to pay. Some of the pastors who duped themselves into believing that they could support general church intents completely out of harmony with local parish objectives, gradually are beginning to raise a feeble voice of protest. The clergy itself is a sleeping giant which could change a secular institution into a sacred enterprise if it could be roused from its complacency and intimidation. The church does not have unity just because quietness prevails, if the reason for the tranquility is that everyone is afraid to speak up. At least, this is not the unity in which Christians should be interested. The only valid unity is a oneness which has as its unifying center something more than the passing whim of currently approved theology. At the heart of Christian unity must be a dynamic interpersonal relationship with Him who is the living Truth.

Jesus was praying for the apostles who had shared His earthly ministry and for all disciples yet to join that little nucleus of early believers. The burden of His heart had to do with unity. "My prayer for them is that they will be of one heart and mind, just as you and I are, Father—that just as you are in me and I am in you, so they will be in us, and the world will believe you sent me" (Jn 17:21, Living Bible). No gnostic illumination is needed to understand what kind of unity is being sought in this prayer. It is oneness where men and women are joined with God in Christ as closely as the Father and the Son are related.

Ask the Ephesians about this oneness. Let them recall for us the heartcry of Paul as he explained to their congregation what he wanted most for them. It was the apostle's cherished dream that they would ultimately "all believe alike about our salvation and about our Saviour, God's Son, and all become full-grown in the Lord—yes, to the point of being filled full with Christ" (Eph 4:13, Living Bible). In the following verse he adds, "Then we will no longer be like children, forever changing our minds about what we believe because someone has told us something different, or has cleverly lied to us and made the lie sound like the truth." Believing alike is important, but the shared belief must have at its heart the Word of God rather than the word of man. Men can be united around a score of vastly differing theological presuppositions, but the oneness is unacceptable if it does not have at its center the historical-experiential Christ of the New Testament.

Ecumenism, as we have seen it rise and fade, is in many ways a burlesque on Christian unity. A lot of obstreperous talk has come from ecumenical councils and groups, which has united some and divided others. In some cases union of groups has evolved without unity of spirit. The results are more than unfortunate. Present emphasis on organic union at the cost of theological or ethical conviction has all but destroyed the conciliar movement. The entire ecumenical organization has probably outlived its usefulness. Other matters are becoming more important and need immediate attention. Structural merger is not imperative; it is not even necessary. Ecumenicity is a quality of spirit unrelated to organic mergers.

So many strange, exotic, pagan-sounding pronouncements have come out of the ecumenical movement that the whole thing has lost its way. It appears that there are a lot of lost sheep trying to be shepherds of a flock of scattered lambs as confused as they. There is one thing around which we do not need or want unity—that is confusion. When the idea prevails that a pluralistic society demands a united church with an unidentifiable core of belief, we are in serious trouble. Such a condition never leads to unity, but to anarchy.

As an evangelical Christian, it is my duty and desire to reach out to my Christian brethren of other communions. No one needs to abandon any conviction or religious principle which he believes to be indispensable in order to have genuine Christian fellowship and cooperation. This kind of ecumenical oneness has little to do with whether I believe bishops stand in the line of apostolic succession or whether I prefer to believe that the church should have no bishops at all. It is not concerned with modes of baptism, liturgies, and rituals. What it does find of crucial significance is a mutual love for Jesus Christ and the spreading of New Testament Christianity into all the world. The circumference is not an essential consideration, only the center.

This does not imply that doctrine is unimportant. But it does mean that the doctrine shall spring directly from the clear teaching of the New Testament itself rather than from some fanciful theory created by men apart from biblical revelation. Our oneness is not simply practical; it must be built on a strong doctrinal basis. No question exists in my mind about the need for a worldwide fellowship of evangelical Christians. Such an international fellowship (not a structured federation of churches necessarily) would provide a platform for speaking to the world with one voice and would open the doors for consultation and mutual understanding. Such a fellowship would not be linked by denominational ties, but by groups and individuals from within all structured churches who share a love for Christ and a dedication to the proclamation of the gospel of salvation. This could be a counterpart to the more liberally oriented ecumenical movement without the faintest desire for organic union of doctrinal bodies.

Where this kind of oneness does not exist, there is adequate reason for multiformity. For a while, evangelicals were afraid of being branded as "polarizers." This is no longer so. Polarization can be a positive good when it distinguishes the living from the dead. As long as the world lasts, some kind of polarization will be unavoidable. The Holy Spirit separates truth from falsehood, bringing comfort to some and condemnation to others. And when Christ returns to earth, polarization will be ultimate, final, and eternal—the saved forever separated from the lost. Truth brings men together. It also divides. Those who love the Truth will gravitate toward their common pole of attraction. Those who reject the Truth will gravitate in the direction of a false pole.

While some people accuse evangelicals of splitting the church (and that is sometimes necessary), I see the more evangelically-oriented disciples of Christ as a tool for discerning the Spirit. There will always be theological liberals and theological conservatives, and never the twain shall meet in any structured union. Why should this be unexpected or unacceptable? The man of the world is not fooled into believing that we are one simply because we constantly talk about unification. The very fact that the situation grows worse the longer we talk about it may convince the outsider that the church is more terribly fragmented than he had thought. The only people we fool are ourselves.

Mainstream Christianity has lapsed into a compromising, tolerant, ecumenical jelly-like substance which attracts no one in this rough-and-ready world. Our design to appease everybody and to be relevant to any kind of philosophical theology has all but annihilated the church. There must be a return to the beliefs which distinguished our forefathers in the faith. Our doctrines must be advocated with unshakeable conviction, and a degree of exclusiveness must be restored to the Christian community. Everything does not belong in the church of Jesus Christ. Of course, everyone is a potential member of the body of Christ, but only on certain conditions prescribed in the New Testament.

The narrow perspective which separates believers on inconsequential matters about which the Scriptures are not clear is to be discouraged. In these cloudy areas, one must be anything but dogmatic. Divisiveness should not be tolerated unless the Bible draws that dividing line for us. Any other polarization stems from the traditions of men and does not warrant sufficient credence to divide us one from another. Many splinter groups have come about over some human tradition which could not be substantiated in any conclusive way by the Scripture. Yet some of the most heated hostilities have surrounded these unyielding positions. We have fought enough over the sovereignty of God and predestination on the one hand and the free will of man on the other. Both truths are included in the Bible. Neither one excludes the other. Likewise, more than an adequate amount of heated debate has flared over conditional and unconditional security. Every man has his preference, to which he is entitled. But he should admit that the Bible is not definitely committed to one view over the other. The same thing can be said for the prescribed method of receiving the Holy Spirit, various modes of baptism, the use of musical instruments in worship, details of prophecy, and the proper version or translation of the Bible.

There is a simple but worthy system for determining what position the church should take. First, what does Jesus say about the issue to be decided? If His words are specific and clear, then I need go no further. My decision is easy enough. Second, if Jesus' word is lacking, is there clarification in the rest of the New Testament? Third, is the suggested position in keeping with the total tenor of the scriptural message, or does it contradict the written Word? Fourth, would the proposed procedure do injustice to the heart of the Great Commission? Fifth, does the concern being recommended detract from the centrality of the work of Christ on the cross and in the empty tomb? There probably are other checklists which would do as well, but this one works for me. By having such a guideline, I am able to keep a more balanced perspective in a time when masses of good people seem unable to recognize any standard of truth.

The structured world organization for ecumenical affairs may have commenced its work a quarter of a century ago with high goals which even included the evangelization of the world. But the years have transformed it until today there is little about the movement that has to do with evangelism. The high goals of ecumenical cooperation have been dissipated into an overanxious effort to create a world church no matter what the cost. Organic union is a goal quite inferior to that of spiritual unity. They are not the same, though both are valid if kept in their proper relationship and sequence of importance.

Neither uniformity nor multiformity is good or bad in itself. Unless there is reason for division, it is normally best to aim for oneness. But when a valid reason is present (a matter of eternal verities), no one should be hesitant about breaking apart from a union which has forfeited its right to unity. It is always better to be divided by truth than united in error. My priority, as it relates to unity and polarity, is a matter of discovering what is truth and then making horizontal relationships amenable to it. Where union serves the cause of truth, my vote is favorable. Where truth is defended by diversity, I have no restraints against being a polarizer.

When I became a Christian over twenty-five years ago, no one questioned the wisdom of polarization between the church and the world. The difference today is in the discernible line of demarcation between the Christian community and the community outside. Two decades ago, no one had any doubt about where the church stood in relation to the world's pagan philosophy. Today the scene has changed.

Now it is not possible to create a polarity between the church and the world without also dividing the church! The reason for this predicament is that the doctrinal and ethical standards of the institutional religious organization have been progressively lowered until the tide of the unregenerate world has washed practically everything into the church. Very grave is the dilemma for Christians when they discover that the commitment of the church is basically no different from that of the unchurched world. When this happens, a polarization inevitably is to be expected inside the organized church, since there is no other way for the Christian community to be separate from the world.

Some there are who shudder at the thought of separation, fearing that such an attitude will encourage Pharisaism. The fundamental principle of separation, however, is not a holier-than-thou disinterest in sinners, but a compassionate concern which constrains us to share our faith in love while at the same time living clean and "unspotted from the world" (Ja 1:27). Paul was referring to this kind of polarity when he wrote, "Come out from among them, and be ye separate" (2 Co 6:17). This advice was given to a local church too intimately aligned with the pagan world. If Paul were alive today, he would give the same admonition to the true and faithful church too closely identified with a false and faithless institution which bears the name but not the nature of Christ.

Study Questions

1. Discuss the distinction between union and unity. Can the church have unity without union? Does union insure unity?
2. Do we need a loose-knit fellowship of evangelicals where varied denominations and groups could work together around a Biblical mission without agreement on peripheral matters? Suggest how such a fellowship might be set up and operated. Who would determine what is peripheral?

3. In what sense can it be argued that our fear of polarization stems from our inability any longer to distinguish between the church and the world?
4. What would you suggest as a general guideline for contending for the truth without being contentious? How can the Christian be unyielding in his convictions without giving the impression of bigotry or lovelessness?

8

Church and State

SO MUCH HAS BEEN WRITTEN about the claims of the church versus the claims of the state that it seems redundant to bring it up again. Regardless of how superfluous the continued discussion of this subject may appear, the issue is far from settled. Anything so controversial of necessity will have to be decided ultimately by each person for himself. Naturally, once the decision is made, every individual has to live with it and accept the consequences for his actions. On the assumption that the balance between one's faithfulness to the church and his loyalty to the state will remain a precarious experience for years to come, perhaps there is room for a bit more discussion.

Christian citizens regularly find themselves oscillating between the authority of the king and the authority of the priest. Most of us love our country and the way of life which it was founded to promote. We want to be loyal supporters of the democratic republic, which is still the grandest of all the world's systems of government. All of us readily admit the weaknesses and the sins of every human government including our own, but some of us still find our land to be the best of all possible worlds. This is particularly true in view of the uncontested fact that no perfect civil system is known or available to mankind. We are forced to choose that which comes nearest to our ideal. Winston Churchill stated appropriately, "Democracy is surely the worst form of government except for all the others that have been tried."

Although my own desire is to be a patriotic citizen, I have no intent to be a chauvinist. Extravagance in anything is risky business, and one does well to give a wide berth to such excesses. But if I do not want to be a chauvinist, neither do I want to be a political chameleon whose attitude toward my country is one of changeable habits and fickle disposition. The least my government can expect from me is that my declared position shall be consistent with my activity. There is no excuse for me if I live in this land of freedom and bounty, enjoy its liberties and plenty, and all the while engage in subversive tactics to undermine the very nation which has supported me. My country owes me something, but I owe my country far more.

At the same time, I am keenly conscious that I am indebted to the church and the way of life which it espouses. Actually, being a Christian means that I am a citizen of two worlds, both of them quite this-worldly. My citizenship within the kingdom of man sometimes demands support which my citizenship in the kingdom of God will not allow. At that point, life bristles with complexities. What does one do in circumstances where he is called upon to deny one loyalty in order to support another? Which does he choose? Is it possible to compromise? If it is, would compromise be Christian or patriotic? These are questions which cause great struggle for many people whose consciences are captive to the Word of God—people like myself who desperately wish to be good citizens of both worlds.

When Paul wrote to the church of Christ in the city of Rome, he was addressing people who lived at the pulsebeat of pagan government. From that very city was to issue the worst persecution against Christians ever known in history. Yet, the apostle instructs those Roman disciples to "be in subjection to the governing authorities. For there is no authority except from God, and those which exist are established by God. Therefore he who resists authority has opposed the ordinance of God; and they who have opposed will receive condemnation upon themselves. For rulers are not a cause of fear for good behavior, but for evil" (Ro 13:1-3, NASB). At the time these words were written, the whole world was living in a state of peace guarded by the empire. This arrangement was endorsed by the Christian apostle. Paul, who knew his Old Testament well, had learned that it is God who gives rulers their place and dispenses His power through them (see Jer 27:5-11; Dan 2:21, 37-38; 4:17). To Paul, the state, pagan though it might have been in its outward manifestations, was God's means of creating some form of order and justice.

The foundation upon which he constructed this concept was the belief that God and the civil ruler are neither opposed to each other nor merged into one, but rather that the state is an instrument by which God rules the world. The sovereignty of God, seen in His use of pagan Cyrus and His authority over Nero, is the ruling conviction which shows through in Paul's writings. A workman's tool may not do as good a job as he would like, but even an imperfect instrument in his hand is better than no tool at all. At times the instrument may mar or even mutilate what the craftsman is working on. Nevertheless, that instrument is in the hand of a skilled master workman whose will controls whatever he may choose to use. In the final analysis, God is in charge, and citizens should respect and honor the rulers through whom He is willing to work, for God is the king's King, too.

A story is told that at the end of the sixteenth century in Scotland, a courageous clergyman named Andrew Melville confronted King James VI, saying, "There are two kings and two kingdoms in Scotland. There is King James, the lord of this commonwealth, and there is Christ Jesus, the King of the church whose subject James the Sixth is, and of whose kingdom he is not a king, nor a lord, nor a head, but a member." And he was right. God is behind the earthly throne and holds final power, and this makes a big difference in my attitude toward kings and governors.

Paul specifically refers to the assessment of taxes, which was as galling then as it is today. Yet, he does not suggest that the yoke of taxation be thrown off, but that it be accepted. To the rulers, whom the apostle calls ministers of God, man is to give tribute for the operation of the seat of government. "Render to all what is due them: tax to whom tax is due; custom to whom custom; fear to whom fear; honor to whom honor" (Ro 13:7, NASB).

To refuse payment of civil tax was considered the same thing as nonfeasance in the area of Christian duty. The Christian is not to be relieved from his obligation to the state on the basis of his obligation to the church. Paul was clearly constructing his recommendation of taxation on the sure word of Jesus, "Render to Caesar the things that are Caesar's, and to God the things that are God's" (Mk 12:17, NASB). When tax collectors asked John the Baptist what they needed to do in response to his preaching of repentance, he did not tell them to get out of their nefarious business, but he demanded, "Collect no more than what you have been ordered to" (Lk 3:13, NASB).

At no time did Jesus defy the authority of Rome. He questioned much of what went on in the name of government as handled by both the Jews and the Romans. That is every citizen's prerogative. But not once did He organize a band of revolutionaries to overthrow the ruling powers. We hear people trying to justify their tactics of subversion and revolution by calling Jesus a revolutionary. What they fail to point out is that Christ was a revolutionary in the realm of man's heart, not in that of governmental affairs, except as conversion of man alters life around him through love and witness. Christ lived within the law of Rome. When He was tried before Pilate, the governor could find absolutely no point at which He had run counter to the imperial throne of Caesar.

No one would argue from these basic principles that there are not specific situations which initiate a real conflict of loyalties. If the state makes demands upon one which his Christian faith forbids him to accept, then the picture has an entirely different setting and needs to be reappraised. In such cases, the disciple must be sure that his disagreement is rooted completely in the word and life of the historical Christ and in the clear teaching of the New Testament. If the conviction is an outgrowth of human tradition, there is no clearcut Christian mandate for disobeying the civil government. But there are situations where the follower of Christ must take his stand against unchristian demands of the state, even if doing so means forfeiting his life.

An illustration from the ancient church is found where two of the disciples were forbidden to speak anymore in the name of Jesus. Peter replied, "Whether it is right in the sight of God to give heed to you rather than to God, you be the judge; for we cannot stop speaking what we have seen and heard" (Ac 4:19-20, NASB). John dramatically warns us against giving obedience to the Antichrist, who opposes the rule of Christ in the world (Rev 13). A later illustration from the third century involved Bishop Cyprian of Carthage who was commanded by Emperor Valerian to sacrifice to the pagan imperial cult. He refused. The proconsul cautioned, "Consider well." The bishop replied, "Execute your orders, the case admits no consideration." Forthwith he was taken away and beheaded.

The issue today is not so much the rejection of the totalitarian state by the Christian church (except in some atheistic regimes), but a rejection of the totalitarian church by the government. That is more than interesting. It is at the least quite shocking. All through history there have been periods and places where some branch of Christendom has tried to rule in civil affairs. The first attempt was under the reign of Constantine, and it was a deadly marriage. Wherever the church has held power over the state, the world has witnessed tragedy. Indeed, the church of Christ has the right and the duty to speak to the state, to condemn its actions when they are wrong, but never to dictate specifically what the rulers must do in any given situation. This is a mutual arrangement by which the state does not interfere in the spiritual realm with earthly legislation. The separation of church and state is built on this principle.

Today, however, the church is encroaching upon the enforcement of legislation. This is a divine mandate which belongs exclusively to the state, and not to the Christian community, which is only a part of the whole. What we now have is a corrupt form of totalitarian Christianity which seeks to rule rather than to serve. The results could be disastrous.

My own priority in this area is twofold. In temporal and civil matters, my mandate is to obey the rulers of my country. In spiritual maters my first and last choice is with the Lord Jesus Christ and the genuine Christian community. Where there is a conflict, my loyalty to Christ always precedes any other. My relationship to the rulers of my country is entirely different from my relationship to the King of kings. Some will insist that this compartmentalizes life into the secular and the sacred. This is hardly true. The two areas—church and state—overlap at points, but they do not duplicate one another. The church has one job to do, and the state has another. Christians must recognize this distinction unless we want to make the two kingdoms into one long before the time for doing so.

When Christ returns, the church will reign with Him over all the kingdoms of the world. Until that time, there is no reason for the church to usurp the authority which belongs to the state or vice versa. If we continue to allow these two kingdoms to have the same objectives this side the consummation of the ages, we can expect nothing but an anemic state and an apostate church.

It is not a question of compartmentalization. It is a question of understanding that the whole consists of its parts. The way to make life whole is not by trying to force everything to do the same job. Completeness comes when each part does what it was made to do in contribution to the welfare of the whole. Therefore, I support my government until it demands my worship. At that point I draw a broad, black, indelible line. That is the one thing which I cannot give to the state. By the same token, I support my church until it demands the role which God has given to the state. Being faithful to God's design for His world is a larger priority than either the civil state or the institutional church.

Study Questions

1. Is there any relationship between being Christian and being patriotic? How does one avoid what happened in Germany when the church embraced Nazi rule out of a sense of rightness? Where is the line to be drawn?
2. What do you believe the Bible means by insisting that Christians be obedient to civil powers? Is there ever a legitimate place for civil disobedience?
3. How far should the church allow the state to go in determining the way man lives? How far should the state allow the church to go?
4. Does the church have the right to reject a totalitarian government? Does the government have the right to reject a totalitarian church?

9

Law and Order

ONCE WE BEGIN THINKING about the political state and man's responsibility to it, the discussion unavoidably turns in the direction of the enforcement of law and the maintenance of order. No subject could be more timely. The whole world has just come through a decade of demonstrations, riots, and anarchy. Defiance of law and order in the name of freedom has been the daily diet of multitudes of both youth and adults.

A seminary president has referred to the last decade as "the silly sixties." Apparently he means that our disorderliness was a foolish and futile attempt to solve problems which require more seasoned judgment and patience than such an approach allowed. While it may be true that the radical revolutionary called attention to some of our social injustices and religious bigotry, it is now generally admitted that not a great deal of practical good came out of that decade of violent reaction to the system of law and order.

Many sober-thinking people would not describe the sixties as silly. For them, those years were too serious for any such adjective. They would choose a word like *shocking*, or *shattering*, or *suicidal*. Indeed, there were times when it looked as if the whole political, legal, educational, and religious structure were going to collapse upon us. But, although the world has been scarred by our mistreatment of the socially-agreed upon legislation which has held us together, God has seen fit to spare us. There is a new mood in the world.

Riots seldom shatter the streets of our cities anymore. Hardly anyone is in a frame of mind to participate in any kind of demonstration. University campuses are strangely quiet, and students have returned to their studies with a more deliberate approach to learning. One almost gets the impression that people are tired, weary with the confusion and instability which characterized the turn of the seventies.

Interestingly enough, today our attention is being turned in a new direction. Masses of people who defended the system of law and order because they could not see its evils, due to the more blatant ugliness of the typical radical, now are taking a new look at the system itself. Political corruption, which has been beneath the skin of society for years, has finally broken through; and the sight has made us all sick to our stomachs.

As long as man lives in his fallenness, he must expect the society which he builds to have decay within it. No sane person would ever assume that Washington and its political or legislative agencies are free from the corruption which inevitably accompanies power. But this awareness must never permit us simply to dismiss the matter as if it were incapable of reform. On the contrary, we should be continually on the alert to such defiance of law and order in high places. And we should raise our voices in protest against it until something is done to correct it.

No people can long survive without law. The first law was given to Adam at the beginning of creation. He was told specifically that he and his wife were not permitted to eat "of the tree of the knowledge of good and evil" (Gen 2:17). Furthermore, he was informed what the penalty would be if the command went unheeded. And, as God had decreed, the punishment promised for disobedience was meted out immediately upon transgression. Thus it is seen that God Himself initiated the system of law and determined its finality.

The first thing God did, as the liberated Hebrews traveled into the wilderness toward their promised land, was to establish a system of law (Ex 20) by which order would be insured for all. In the following chapters of the book of Exodus, numerous laws for the protection of all were given to Moses by Jehovah. Without law and order, it would have been impossible for the people to have survived.

Reciprocity is at the core of all humane law. Sometimes we forget this. Law provides a mutually arranged method of cooperation through which everyone should benefit. Since the men who make the laws are imperfect creatures, it is to be expected that the system itself will have its weaknesses. Because of this fact, injustices develop. It is at these points of inconsistency that the populace must rise up to protest vigorously. Such protest should be for the purpose of redressing a specific wrong, however, and not for the purpose of destroying all law and order. Regardless of what kind of law may prevail, there will always be problems connected with it. But where there is no law, or where each man decides his own, society is in shambles.

Most empires of world grandeur throughout history have not been murdered from without so much as they have committed suicide from within. The visible cause of defeat has been the invaders who forced submission onto the conquered peoples. But, in practically every instance, the internal decay of the will had done its work long before the alien forces arrived. Our worst enemy is our loss of will to be a great nation. And what is said of the country of which I am a part may be said of essentially every other land. The desire for greatness is almost a thing of the past with most civilized nations.

This loss of will for continued greatness as a nation under God is a serious thing. Nothing could be more tragic for our way of life. Many of the radicals were ready to throw everything to the four winds in exchange for the joy of the present moment. For them, there was no tomorrow. Likewise, great numbers of the quieter folk have felt the hopelessness of a world of chaos where law means nothing and where there are no absolutes by which to live. Across the world there is a sense of impending doom which has caused some to become hedonists, others to develop into wild anarchists, and still others to sit idly, waiting for the coming of the Lord!

The hour has come when man must come clean with God and his fellows. If the law is going to be binding on the common man, then it must be binding also on the politicians, statesmen, and legislators. We can have no double standard. No people will honor a law which exempts some and regulates others. The judge must live by the same laws by which the little people abide. From the poorest shanty to the chief executive's mansion, the law must be equally binding and equally enforced.

We have tampered with the underpinning of justice. With corruption in high places as well as violation of law among the average citizenry, we are precariously near to having removed the support upon which society rests. There is a sound of cracking foundations; and we find ourselves either weeping bitterly or laughing loudly in effort to cover up the sound of a collapsing world.

When Paul exhorts the followers of Christ to "be subject to principalities and powers, to obey magistrates" (Titus 3:1), he is approving a system of law and order. But it is an unwritten and universally accepted fact that rulers are to be above reproach themselves if they are to demand the obedience of their subjects. A similar arrangement is obvious in the command, "Honour thy father and thy mother" (Ex 20:12). Unquestionably, if a parent is to be honored, he must be honorable! No child can honor a father or mother who lives a dishonorable life. In the same manner, no citizen can long obey political rulers whose lives are examples of corruption. Public office is a sacred trust. Too often it is exploited for ends other than that of serving the people.

If it is true that man cannot obey public officials who break the law themselves, it is clearly manifest that there is a place where dissent becomes necessary. Every individual must be guaranteed that right. Such dissent should take the form of public debate rather than open violence. We have seen violence used, but it has done more harm than good. From the earliest days of our nation, we have elected representatives to discuss issues which concern us and to register our opinions. Nonetheless, it is not at all unusual for citizens to fail to write or call their representatives in numbers vast enough to inform them of the prevailing feeling in our community.

Law is never an end in itself. It must be a means to an end, and that end must be the good of *all* people. Legislators and the common man must work together in creating a system of law which is as fair to all groups as is humanly possible. Every man's rights are to be handled with due regard to others around him. When injustice is believed to be present, it should be exposed and corrected. No stone should be left unturned for fear of bringing the wickedness of prominent persons to light. When public officials are derelict in their duties, or when they use their positions for selfish ends, they must be brought to justice and put out of office.

If a man's priority lies in his relationship to Jesus Christ, he will monitor his attitude and actions relating to the state in much the same manner as did the Master. Jesus never resorted to violence in order to protect Himself or to free Israel from the oppressive rule of despised Rome. He did not get embroiled with the political structures except to verbally condemn them where they were wrong. Our Lord was crucified because He upset the religious establishment; but even at His trial, He refrained from hostilities and abuse.

We do well to live within the law as we voice our objections to the right people. We ought also to be a part of the struggle to clean house in political structures for the sake of those who are shortchanged by the inequities of any and all human systems. In so doing, we help create a climate in which the world will recognize its duty to God, the Creator of all systems of law and order.

It has been suggested that respect for law is the religion of liberty. If democracy is to survive as a way of life in the West—if it is to be spread into areas of the human community where men are under terrible totalitarian pressures—we must learn to retain a balance between freedom and order. We cannot afford to suppress man's democratic freedom for the purpose of establishing order, but neither can we afford to ignore law and order in the effort to insure freedom. It is a delicate balance. Yet, it is an absolute imperative.

To watch Jesus Christ on the pages of the New Testament is to see a Man who lived in the midst of all the complexities of a world system which was as corrupt as any before or since. He dwelt among corrupt politicians, charlatan churchmen, cutthroats, and thieves, as well as among average citizens in Israel who covered up their dishonesty with the powder of decency. Hardly a day passed when He was not engaged in exposing this sickness of His time. But it is very important to note that Jesus was able to experience complete freedom while at the same time refusing to use His "rights" to defy what law and order existed in the Roman Empire and the Jewish state.

Not one of us can claim to be Christ's equal. He is the perfect man, the embodiment of all that is true and good. But He is our example, and we do ourselves eternal damage when His manner of life is not established as our pattern. As Christians, we all need to look carefully at the way our Lord handled Himself in the midst of the crime and corruption of the first century, and then set ourselves to the task of confronting society's system of law and order in the same manner. At this point, every person has to establish his own honest, Christlike criteria for action. "The disciple is not above his master: but everyone that is perfect shall be as his master" (Lk 6:40).

Study Questions

1. In what sense is it true that law is compulsory in any society involving more than two people? Why must there be law?
2. It is said that law originated with God. What relationship can be found between divine law and contemporary legislation? How can one be certain which laws are endorsed by God and which are not?
3. Crime and corruption are found at every level of society. How can the country go about restoring respect for the law when so much deceit and corruption is being revealed in high places of government?
4. How would you evaluate the concept of law and order as held by Jesus? If He were bodily present in the twentieth century, do you think He would act in the same manner as He did in the first? Explain your answer.

10

Justice and Discrimination

Is IT NOT REASONABLE to state that the first act of discrimination and injustice was that which took place between the sons of Adam? As far as we are able to ascertain, the root of the injustice had nothing to do with race (they had the same parents), or with social prestige, or with affluence and poverty, or with minority status. Abel was discriminated against because his sacrifice was accepted by God, and Cain's was not. The older brother could not see any justice, so he engaged himself in a plan to balance things in his own favor. That is what usually happens when a fight for justice begins. Everybody is selfishly oriented, and whatever the outcome, there is still injustice somewhere.

No stronger measures to bring justice have ever been adopted than those used by Cain. Feeling that God had discriminated in favor of his brother, Cain decided that counter-discrimination against Abel was the solution. So he killed him (Gen 4:3-8). Abel appears to have been completely innocent. God is thought to have been unjust with Cain, and Cain was ostensibly unjust with Abel. It is always the innocent who get hurt in the fight for justice. Not often do we go as far as Cain in our desire to see justice carried out, but even that has been known to happen.

Originally, God tried to keep all people together without dividing them into nations and races. But it did not work, and the Creator was forced to separate the peoples into allotted areas on the earth where they spoke a tongue all their own and developed a culture uniquely theirs (see Gen 11). As civilization advanced and means of transportation became more easily accessible, people migrated from one place to another. In our cosmopolitan areas, there are segments of peoples from many races and lands. The world itself has become a melting pot. Yet, people and groups who leave their native habitats still become victims of discrimination, even after generations of them have lived in the nation to which they have immigrated.

As man's ethical conscience developed, he began to see that this situation was far from right. In America, the struggle to do something about injustice began when the abolitionists demanded that black slavery be terminated. It took a civil war to settle that issue, and even then discrimination was not eliminated. Much hatred was generated by the emancipation of the Blacks; hostility between North and South was no worse than that exercised between masters and slaves. Across the intervening years, the resentment has been expressed by continued discrimination against and deprivation of the black man. As other minority groups arrived in the United States, the prejudice included them as well.

The struggle for equality has gained momentum as the ethnic minorities have called attention to their grievances against the predominant community. Each year the demands are increased, as more and more of their claims are granted by society. Much of this excessive handout policy has been generated by a mushrooming guilt induced by a propagandizing cadre sympathetic to the minority causes. Compensatory programs have been worked out which even demand that financial reparations be made to settle past accounts of injustice. Everyone is aware of the issues. Some continue to keep the fires burning, while others try to put them out. Great numbers both of the minority groups and of the larger population have grown weary of the excess mileage which has been derived from the cries of social, political, and economic injustice.

Special interest groups, each with its own claims of injustice, are now vying with the minorities to have their voices heard. Women's Liberation aims to free females from all the old customs and morals which they claim have enslaved them to the male chauvinists. And now the gay liberation movement cries for social acceptance in the free world. And there are others.

What is justice? Can there ever be justice for all people? Is it possible to get rid of discrimination altogether? If so, how long is it going to take, and what is it going to cost in life, property, and relationships? These are all legitimate questions. Where does the Christian fit into this maze of confusion? Does the Bible offer any light? What did Jesus say about it? These questions also are valid.

The prophets of the eighth century B.C. in Israel were incensed at the lack of social justice in the land. The leaders of Israel and the rich of the land were exploiting the poor, taking advantage of widows and orphans, and totally ignoring their ethical obligations to the less fortunate. They hoped that God would accept their sacrifices and overlook their acts of injustice. Micah was emphatic in his insistence that God cannot be bribed. "He has told you what he wants," writes the prophet, "and this is all it is: *to be fair and just and merciful, and to walk humbly with your God*" (Mic 6:8, Living Bible).

Jesus' parable about the good Samaritan (Lk 10:30-37) was a pointed effort to break down the artificial walls of discrimination between the Jews and their mixed-blooded relatives. Not only did the Master clarify the way to be a good neighbor; He explicitly stated that race had absolutely nothing to do with it. When He spoke to the Syrophoenician woman in seemingly harsh words, it is almost certain that

He was quoting a Jewish aphorism for the purpose of showing how absurd it is to reject a needy person because he happens to be born in a different race (Mk 7:25-29). John was positive that the love of God could not dwell in the heart of any man who "shutteth up his bowels of compassion" (1 Jn 3:17) toward a single person needing his help. Surely that understanding of mercy would have been unchanged by ethnic or religious background. And the whole concept was closely related to our concern with social and economic justice.

Clearly manifest to the thinking Christian is the relationship between human justice and divine love. God's mercy and compassion are lavishly poured upon us all. Some reject the love of God and make an irrevocable mess of their lives. When this happens, it does no good to cry "injustice!" Some of us accept that divine love but hoard it for ourselves. We may even decide that we are more deserving than others—that men who do not have the blessings which we enjoy just are not worthy of them. Others receive the unmerited favors of earth and selflessly share them with those who are less blessed. This use of the Lord's bounties is the only one that is entitled to be called Christian.

It should be pointed out that, while the Christian ethic does prescribe personal sharing with the needy and concern for the deprived, the structuring of society on a level where everyone has an equal share is not demanded or recommended. The ancient church did hold all things communally for a while (Ac 2:44-47), but the equalizing of men by a community underwriting of needs was confined to those within the church. They alone would have a center of mutual dedication and love strong enough to prompt such an existence for any length of time. Acts of a selfish nature were dealt with most severely (Ac 5:1-11). And it should be noted that even among Christians the plan soon aborted because it was basically unrealistic. A genuine communal life of equal sharing would require either that we be perfect beings or that there be continuous supervising and policing tactics.

Man's initiative, motivation, and ability must be brought into the picture. God never intended that a world full of unredeemed, selfish people would disregard these factors in the business of living. Man is foolish if he expects more of fallen men than God expects. The system of private enterprise is to be preferred to any other form of government, since it alone makes room for these innate differences in people. Therefore, it alone is realistic. This is not an endorsement of selfishness. Every form of social life known to mankind has its flaws and its selfish ends. It is the recognition of ambition which merits some degree of reward. We must not stifle initiative. When that is gone, we do not have justice, though we may have equality. What we are left with is stagnation.

While insisting that all classes and races of men need one another and must learn to live in reciprocal relationships, Jesus suggested that real justice may have to wait for the next world. There are persons who will become defensive at this point, as though the life to come is of no concern to them. They will be happy with nothing less than justice *now*. We should remember that not even the Son of God was spared a share in this world's injustice and discrimination. In the story of the rich man and Lazarus, our Lord points out that the divine way of balancing the scales often is weighted on one side in this life (Lk 16:19-31).

Christ was definitely not sanctioning discrimination and injustice. He was only telling it straight. For us to wage war against these evils within our social order is to have His blessing. However, we may go too far and become irrationally possessed by dreams of a utopia not possible for a fallen world. The Master was not so much encouraging the poor man to be content with the idea of reparation in heaven as He was warning the rich man that every man must face his own judgment. It must also be pointed out that the minority group individual is not assured of heaven because he is among the persecuted. That is not what the story in Luke's gospel is saying to us. It is announcing that God, from whom nothing of motivation and intent is concealed, is the only One who can and will create an order of justice where there is no discrimination.

If the whole world could be made fully Christian, that which man dreams of would become reality. By this I am not intimating that things would be different if everyone joined the church. Not all people in the institutional church are Christian. What I am talking about is the kind of society described in the Bible as the coming reign of Christ at the end of this world order. Isaiah says of that day, "He will rule with perfect fairness and justice from the throne of his father David. He will bring true justice and peace to all nations of the world" (Is 9:7, Living Bible). Until the Saviour returns to establish the kind of reign Isaiah described, there is actually no known way to rid the world of discrimination and injustice. Social justice is not possible as long as our hearts are dishonest. Basing his hopes on Psalms 82, 85, and 86, John Milton conjured an image of the coming day of divine justice.

> The Lord will come and not be slow,
> His footsteps cannot err;
> Before him righteousness shall go,
> His royal harbinger.
> Truth from the earth, like to a flower,
> Shall bud and blossom then;
> And justice, from her heavenly bower,
> Look down on mortal men.

Legislation may help, but it is no solution. Love cannot be legislated, and without love there is no justice deserving of the name. Inevitably, persons and groups discriminated against utilize the law in such a way that, once their declared rights are protected, the rights of some other group are denied. Discrimination and injustice are not canceled out. They are only swapped from one to another. Maybe this juggling game is the best we can do in a society as complex and incurably evil as ours. Sophocles said appropriately, "There is a point at which even justice is unjust."

One fact offers us some hope for this world. Sooner or later, men begin to realize how ineffectual are their demonstrations, legislation, and acts of violence. Therefore, instead of wasting time and energy in marches, exhibitions, shouting, and lobbying, which only create a lot of noise and stir up even more hostility, I have committed myself to another method. Being fully convinced that a vital, living relationship with Jesus Christ kills the monster of injustice, I have dedicated my life to leading men and women to His feet. If justice can be increased in the land, it will be done as individuals come one by one under the transforming power of the living Lord. Knowing Him who is the source of love implants within the human heart a good will toward men that removes personal injustice.

Becoming a Christian does not render one incapable of discrimination. In a sense, becoming a Christian increases one's powers of discrimination. The very word has been given a bad sound because of its association with racism. But it is a good word. To discriminate is to distinguish between opposites. It is to divide the good from the best, perceiving that which is invaluable to attaining the highest life. This means that the Christian inevitably will be more careful in the choice of his friends and companions, but that he will love and respect as human beings even those with whom he has little social affinity. To put it in biblical terms, Christians will be "wise as serpents, and harmless as doves" (Mt 10:16).

What we need is not sweeping social change, development of countercultures, creation of alternative lifestyles, or even humanization of society. These are all shallow, short-lived remedies for a problem that is not touched by such measures. What the world needs is that which the evangelical refers to as conversion. Justice is directly related to conversion. Man is unjust by nature because he puts himself first. Not until he discovers the expulsive power of a new affection does he learn to love others above himself. My priority, therefore, is far more than a struggle for justice. That is to treat symptoms, and brings only temporary relief. My priority, rather, is the search for personal conversion from sin and self. That is to get at the source of the whole problem.

Study Questions

1. Without referring to a dictionary, define justice. Is it humanly possible to create a society where there is no injustice?
2. What, in your opinion, is the area of greatest discrimination in the world today? Is there discrimination in your neighborhood? Is there any in your church? What can you do to help alleviate these problems?
3. What place does love have in the contemporary struggle for justice? Can there be justice without love? Can lasting justice be legislated?
4. Does Christian conversion automatically solve the problem of personal discrimination against others? Validate your answer from your own experience as well as that of others you know. Were the apostles ever guilty of discrimination?

11

War and Peace

WHAT SHOULD BE the Christian's attitude toward war? Does being a Christian mean that all forms of war are henceforth outlawed? Or can one engage in military combat and be loyal to the Christian ethic at the same time? And if a man feels that his conscience objects to war, can he give patriotic service to his country in other ways? Can he work in a munitions plant or in any other industrial complex where items are manufactured to be used in military service? These questions are only the beginning of the quandries invading the minds of men and women who are reevaluating the church's response to war. But they are at least a place to start.

Only once in recorded history has war been outlawed on a universal basis when it really worked. That was during the days of the Roman Empire, and the condition was known as the *Pax Romana*. It is more than a coincidence that Jesus lived during this phase of the ancient world's peaceful reign. Some believe that it was Christ more than Caesar who was responsible for the absence of war. He is called in Scripture "the Prince of Peace" (Is 9:6), and at His return the second time a thousand years of peace is promised (Rev 20: 1-3). No contradiction appears, strange as it may seem to some, between His peaceful rule and the war led by Christ against wickedness which brings about the millenial reign (see Rev 19:11-21).

Whatever may be said about the Roman peace, it must be pointed out that the condition existed not because a law against war was declared, but because the Roman armies were so strong. No one dared attack from the forces of world rule when it was evident that to do so would be national suicide. Great armies were stationed over all the conquered territories to discourage any kind of revolt. The point I am making is that there was no federation of nations that legislated to outlaw war. On the contrary, the peoples of the nations had no voice in the matter. Rome simply announced the arrangement and pledged herself to enforce world peace for the benefit of all. Peace then was constructed on the solid rock of military strength which made war by any farflung segment of the empire an unthinkable thing.

Today the situation is vastly different and yet quite similar. There is no world empire to insure peace by the threat of annihilation. Instead, two great military nations exist with opposing political ideologies. Each of these has its allies scattered around the world. Freedom from global war has been rendered possible since World War II by the precarious balance of power retained between these two military giants. It is my conviction that the United Nations would be of no value in keeping the world from a nuclear holocaust if this balance was not guarded by both empires.

It is the nature of man to fight. There is something of the brute savage within him. No amount of civilization removes that from his nature. Only the indwelling presence of the Prince of Peace can alter man's warring madness. And even then, his humanity is not canceled. Therefore, the tendency toward loyalty to a threatened cause will show itself far from dead. Should a third world war break out, even those who now are decrying the continued emphasis on military preparedness will be caught up in the conflict.

While it is both sane and commendable to work for peace, it may be insane to act as though the problem of war finally can be solved by excusing oneself from participating in the defense of peace. War will not go away just because we say it is naughty, carry placards denouncing it, or refuse the draft. There always will be men and women who do not see combat as the worst possible evil, who refuse to parade for what they consider to be a questionable peace, and who deplore the thought of objecting to military duty. And as long as such people exist, there will be war. The refusal to accept one's place in a factious world is probably the one thing which will precipitate conflict most quickly. We fool ourselves if we think there are not hordes of unprincipled men ready to take advantage of peace-loving people and national programs of disarmament.

Peace is never a gift. It is earned. We hear a good bit of talk among military personnel about winning the war. A much higher goal is that of winning the peace. And yet, there is an undeniable relationship between these two expressions. It is by winning wars that peace is won. Peace must not be equated only with the absence of fighting. Had the United States and her allies preferred the kind of peace which some are advocating today (evasion of open confrontation) in either of the world wars, the consequences could have been tragic. The peace resultant from noninvolvement would have been slavery. And precisely the same thing must be said in response to the argument against our being involved in protecting weak nations from the ruthless spread of communist aggression against their will.

Peace without honor is not peace at all. Peace without freedom is likewise a counterfeit. There are some conditions far worse than war. In times of war, at least men are fighting for something very dear to them, usually freedom for themselves and their families. When one's freedom is taken from him and he is not allowed to protest his loss, the suppression results in the worst living conditions imaginable.

To know that loved ones are threatened with oppression

by alien forces ready to torture or even to kill them is more than enough to justify some aspects of war. I cannot assume that being a Christian demands that I reject involvement in military combat, when such negating action on my part would endanger the lives and freedom of others. After all, if it is wrong to take arms to kill an enemy, it is equally wrong to refuse to use arms to save the life of a friend. Either way there is suffering and death. The sin of omission is no less fatal in such a case than is the sin of commission.

Those who disclaim the nation's right to bear arms may be too idealistic, unless they want capitulation on the part of that nation. The buildup of weaponry should not be escalated beyond that which is needed to guarantee peace. But the point of tapering must remain a variable which depends on many contingencies. Negotiations for peace always are in order, even when the peace table looks like a fickle arrangement. Ultimately, the best deterrent to war is a well-supplied arsenal. The knowledge that such a system of weaponry exists and is operable at any given moment is security than which there is none better.

When the Christian church begins to tell the state what it should do in specific military situations, the religious community has usurped a right which does not belong to it. The Christian is to be a light in the darkness of a wicked world. But he is not to be a blowtorch trying to enlighten men with a vicious flame. His light is to be gentle and pervasively contagious. In the same way, the composite fellowship of these individual Christians is not to attempt to scorch the hide of government and military leaders by demanding that they accept the light of Christian ethics.

Pronouncements from church councils in which all war is condemned unilaterally and the state is served with a notice as to what it must do are irresponsible solutions to a monstrous ill. Nonmilitary persons are totally unequipped to do more than suggest the general Christian code of ethics as a guideline for national policy. Only men trained in the field of warfare know the situations confronted on the battlegrounds. And only the person engaged in higher levels of national defense is capable of having a full view of the complicated ordeal of balancing peace and security.

The question is not whether war is right or wrong. War is never right, but it may be less wrong than its alternative. This is what is meant by a just war. There are times and conditions which make war the most just action for all involved. Not to enter into conflict under such circumstances would be an injustice uncalled for. A just war is better than an unjust peace. I would always prefer that freedom-loving people should ask why I supported a just war than why I did not.

A just war is one which is clearly the best choice between two or more possible courses of action. To defend the weak from the strong, when the latter's objective is to destroy or enslave the weak, is an example of a just war. To be an aggressor in the initiation of a military combat dedicated to selfish ends would be unjust in anybody's ethic. The problem is to know when the conflict begins to take on the hues of selfishness. Yet, every man has to make that decision. Blind patriotism is a crime against God and man. Patriotism may be a boon to all if it is enlightened by both reason and conscience. We must rid ourselves of the presupposition that it is always evil to support armed conflict.

Probably no one is one hundred percent consistent one hundred percent of the time. Ours is an imperfect society. But often one who opposes all war as immoral will resort to violence to support his position. Some of the young men who reject the draft will not hesitate to engage in street or campus riots. This type of dialectic is common today.

A good example of this inconsistency is demonstrated by Dietrich Bonhoeffer. Although Bonhoeffer rejected the killings of war, yet he participated in a plot to murder Adolph

Hitler while at the same time preaching against the use of armed force.

We would find it difficult to censor Bonhoeffer for sharing in a plan to assassinate the man responsible for the brutal massacre of millions. It would seem that this would have been an example of choosing the lesser of two wrongs. Yet consistency from his point of view would have called for a different course of action. It is difficult to comprehend how a man could be a proponent of the "no war under any conditions" theory, and yet try to kill another human being. The declared position and the declared deed should fit together. A much better stance would have been to state clearly his objection to killing, but to admit that society is far too imperfect for one to be consistent in his refusal to be involved in the conflict.

The Old Testament is filled with the accounts of wars in which God Himself is said to have had a hand. Concluding the New Testament is a writing which is every bit as militaristic as any book written during the dispensation of law. Some argue that John's vision in Revelation should not be in the canon of Christian Scripture at all. This is due to our lopsided concept of God as loving, but never judging. Some also have insisted that the God of Jesus is not the same as the God of Joshua. That, of course, is a heresy condemned by the early church. The fact is that God appears not only to permit war but to engage in it Himself. According to John, God will close out the age with a vicious war under His direct supervision.

When the soldiers asked John the Baptist what was ethically expected of them if they were to be ready for the kingdom of heaven which he had announced, he replied, "Do not take money from anyone by force, or accuse anyone falsely, and be content with your wages" (Lk 3:14, NASB). This advice was given along with similar guidance for the tax collectors. What was prescribed in both cases was a prohibition against extortion and violent injustice. Nothing was said which would insinuate that either the system of taxation or that of military service should be abandoned. No nation can long survive without some form of both.

As the tide of public opinion turned against Him and it became clear to Jesus that He was soon to suffer, the Master turned to the disciples with a word of warning. Since He soon would be taken from them, it would become imperative that they learn to face a hostile world without the physical presence of their Lord. Among the things which were suggested as needful was a sword. "Let him who has no sword sell his robe and buy one" (Lk 22:36, NASB). The sword would not be used in defending Jesus (see Jn 18:10-11), since the crucifixion was ordained by God. Certainly there was no intent of aggression such as that which characterized the Christian church in the days of the Holy Crusades. This was contrary to the whole spirit of Christ. But, in view of the kind of world they would have to face after His death, the disciples would have to be ready to defend themselves.

Later in this discourse with His disciples, Jesus seems to react against the reply of the anxious zealots, "Lord, look, here are two swords" (Lk 22:38, NASB). In their readiness to defend Him or wage war in His name, they had missed His point. However, we must not rule out the possible use of the sword in self defense in the event of persecution. If the disciples had done so, the Christian movement might have been put to death before it had a chance to get into the world.

No one knows what Jesus would have done if He had been drafted to serve in the military forces of His day. There were no wars anyway. I think that probably He would have been obedient to the state, but He would have accepted death at the hands of enemy forces rather than inflict it Himself in personal defense. He who laid down His life for us on the cross would have done no less on some other field of battle. Of course, that was not in the Father's will for His life; therefore, our discussion of such a variation in the divine plan is purely hypothetical.

The woman caught in adultery was brought to Jesus with the reminder that the law called for her death (see Jn 8:1-11). Had they proceeded to kill her as she lay at His feet, would Christ have engaged in open conflict against them? Would He have shielded her and died with her, or would He have fought them with His own hands? What would He say to us should we be caught in such an exigency? And what does our assumed answer say about our involvement in a war fought to protect the weak and innocent?

War and peace in many ways are two sides of the same coin. They are conditions so interwoven that at times it is impossible to separate them without destroying peace altogether. In a fallen world there can be no uninterrupted peace. What peace we do have is won by war. To be sure, that peace is mingled with terrible suffering and sorrow. We would like to have it otherwise. But that is a part of the consequences of man's sin, and we will live with it until the King comes with a divine sceptre of universal peace and justice.

My priority is peace. Absence of war is not always the best peace for all persons involved. I want no peace which dishonors free men, cancels hope, or stifles the spirit. Death is much preferred to that. Unless I can breathe deeply, speak freely, and live with dignity, there is no peace even though the guns are silent. When war is the only way left to insure peace with honor, then war becomes the expedient for achieving that peace.

Study Questions

1. It is said that it is man's nature to fight. Is this true? If so, why? What can be done to change his nature? Does it work?

2. Does the concept of a just war have any meaning for you? Clarify what such a war would be, how it would be fought, and what its objectives would be.
3. Is peace among nations ever given or is it always earned? Does your answer imply that winning even a temporary peace may require an engagement in war? Does it mean that negotiations can bring universal peace?
4. Will the world ever be free of war? Will we have to wait for the millennium? What should we do about war and peace in the meantime?

12

Sex and Family

IN RECENT YEARS we have been witnessing a moral revolution. Morality is at an alltime low. Taboos have been set aside. Sex is talked about freely and engaged in casually. Fornication and adultery are old fashioned words which have lost their stigma. Other terms are used to describe the old sins without admitting that there is anything wrong with the practice of them. Premarital and extramarital sex are the more sophisticated designations given to sexual experience outside the marriage bond. Nowhere does the Bible use three euphemisms; it employs the older definitive words implying guilt and shame.

Several of the mainline denominations of Christendom have gone on record condoning sexual relations for single persons. Others more cautious have adopted a more liberal viewpoint toward sexual promiscuity than they held in the past. Sin seldom is considered a factor in sexual expression, unless human relationships are injured in the experience. What these relationships are that possibly could be *uninjured* is hard to imagine. Advocators of the new morality are insisting that no act is wrong unless it is against nature. And the sticky problem seems to be that no one is quite sure what nature actually is. Thus the concept of moral sin has become so fluid that it shifts with the newest announcement as to what natural sexuality may be.

Permissiveness has become a way of life, and it has affected every facet of the world's existence. Naturally, the most intimate of human relationships would not be expected to go unscathed. Man does not like restrictions placed on him by law or by social custom. He refuses to be happy as long as these authoritarian codes hamper him. As a consenting adult who can find another who shares his desires, he demands that he be free to do what he wishes without societal rejection or discrimination.

It was not infrequent to find men in the early church who looked upon all sex as fundamentally bad and who made unwilling exceptions only for procreation. Gradually, sex within marriage became more acceptable, but it was not the kind of thing one talked about with any openness. In later times the tenor was changed so that sex came to be emphasized as wholly good, a gift of the Creator, with no stigma at all. From there it has been but a short step to declaring that if sex is good, then it can never be bad. Yet there is quite a difference in saying that sex is basically good because it is a gift of God and in saying that it cannot be bad. This opens the door to practically any kind of laxity, moral deviation, and perversion of the purpose of sexuality.

Sigmund Freud believed that a major cause of emotional illness was to be found in the indoctrination by the church which led people to a denial of sexual expression. Sexual repression created a sense of emotional bondage which in turn produced most of the human being's hangups. Out of this concept developed the teaching that the superstitious belief that sex desire is stimulated by the devil must be discarded. When guilt is purged and one is liberated from his old inhibitions, his life will become less rigid and more at ease. He will be able to adjust to the normal cravings of physical appetite with no need for unnatural suppression. And the modern world has carried this idea about as far as it will go.

The current craze for freedom from traditional restraints has unleashed a monster of passion upon civilization. Sex is used to sell practically every known commodity. It is featured in nearly all the entertainment media: movies, television, stage plays. Publishing interests have given themselves over to a lucrative display of sex. Most best-sellers are sex books, and the corner newsstands are deluged with lewd and pornographic materials available even to the youngest children. And the final bastion against immorality has capitulated at last, and we are hearing irresponsible sex talk in church councils and conferences as well as reading disgraceful articles in religious periodicals condoning sexual looseness.

We are approaching the point of sex saturation which is making the whole exploitation of promiscuous sex between men and women a bit nauseous. This may be a part of the explanation for the widespread interest in aberrant forms of sexual expression. One of man's basic drives is that of sex, but when the need is supplied to excess, he grows restless in the desire to find new and exciting ways to do an old thing. Hence the uninhibited pursual of uncivilized and barbaric forms of animalistic sexuality.

Now we have communal sex styles for the unmarried in which young people live together with several others plus the offspring from the group. Group parentage is the pattern, and the normal father—mother—child relationship is being abandoned. Sex communes are not as prevalent as they once were, however, precisely because they do not satisfy the innate one-man-one-woman-for-life design for which human beings were created.

Still with us are the old forms of fornication and adultery mentioned earlier. Since the beginning of the human drama there have been experimenting individuals who attempt to obtain the benefits of marriage without the responsibilities. And there always have been married persons who add a little spice to their humdrum home life with an affair on the side. Marriage itself is entered into with a far less sense of sacredness and permanence than has been the case in past generations. Divorce is easy to procure, and hardly anyone objects to remarriage as often as convenient.

Added to this is the changing attitude toward marriage and childbearing. With sexual intercourse readily accessible, and with its growing acceptability outside the marriage bond, many young people see nothing to be gained by a ceremony which takes away their freedom. Contraceptives now can be purchased by teenagers, and an abortion is not hard to arrange if necessary. And with the talk about population explosion, many are encouraged to turn to contraceptives and abortions with the notion that they are helping solve a serious sociological and ecological menace. The thought of sin never enters into their minds.

Nowhere does the Bible outlaw the use of contraceptives or the regulation of the size of families. But medical and mechanical devices in a time of declining moral conscience can become an excuse for promiscuity and can cause the breakdown of family living. The founding of the National Birth Control League in 1913 was a good move in that the dissemination of medical—moral information was greatly needed. But it opened the door to a concentration upon sex for sex's sake in the minds of many persons who are not mature enough to handle the responsibility generated by the utilization of birth control methods. With the almost foolproof means of prevention and termination of pregnancies, numerous ethicists are now playing down the biblical prohibition of premarital and extramarital relationships.

A word needs to be included here about abortion, since the irresponsible attitude of some churchmen toward the abrupt ending of human life is far more evasive than it is helpful. Talk about unacceptable pregnancy as a reason for the consideration of an abortion says nothing. An unacceptable pregnancy could be anything from a real risk to the life of an expectant mother to the rejection of an illicitly conceived life. Only a few would question a therapeutic abortion when a mother's life is endangered. Most of us would sanction a surgical cathartic of the uterine cavity following a forced rape. When X rays prove conclusively that an unborn child is hopelessly deformed and retarded, there is also reason for moral and medical concurrence in the decision to abort the life cycle. In my opinion, these exceptions should be prescribed as the limits placed on abortion. We have no right to terminate any life, born or unborn, simply because it is unwanted or unacceptable to us.

Homosexuality is one of the most serious of moral problems in modern times. The practice of such abnormal acts has been around since earliest days, possibly since the days of Noah (see Gen 9:20-27). Sodomy definitely was a problem in the days of Abraham (Gen 19:1-11). For several millenia the practice of homosexuality (and lesbianism) was branded as sin pure and simple. Such persons were considered worse than animals and were denied recognition by society. Within the last hundred years we have come more and more to see this deviant form of sex as an illness like alcoholism.

Homosexuality is both a sin and a sickness. The balance between the two varies with the individual case. Within the last fifty years we have begun to feel the persuasive powers of liberalism from the European continent, a liberalism which has undercut practically everything formerly held to be sacred or evil. Only of late, however, have we commenced to say that there is neither a serious moral nor a medical problem at this point. The trend today is to say that such persons must be accepted simply as preferring a sexual lifestyle which is as normal for them as is heterosexuality for others. On this basis, homosexuals are received into the membership of the church. And there is reason to assume that they will soon be granted access to pulpits and classrooms as pastors and teachers. Homosexuality is said to be as normal as left-handedness.

It is my unshakeable conviction that homosexuals must be accepted as having sacred worth and must be granted every civil and human right given to any other person. Christians should accept them as individuals and make every effort to bring them to Christ, who can transform them from darkness into light. But homosexuals should not be granted membership in the Christian church unless they give evidence of the new birth and dedicate themselves to a rigorous discipline which disallows the practice of their old habit. Members of the body of Christ must be changed from what they were, and the change must be clearly begun at the moment of admission into that body. This has been the stance of the community of faith since the days of the New Testament (see 1 Co 5).

The Word of God is explicit at the point of sexual sin as it relates to a perversion of the divine plan. Speaking of those who engage in such life styles, Paul says,

> Even their women turned against God's natural plan for them and indulged in sex with each other. And the men, instead of having a normal sex relationship with women, burned with lust for each other, men doing shameful things with other men, and as a result, getting paid within their own souls with the penalty they so richly deserved. They were fully aware of God's death penalty for these crimes, yet they went right ahead and did them anyway, and encouraged others to do them, too (Ro 1:26-27, 32, Living Bible).

In the letter to the debauched Corinthians are found these words: "Don't fool yourselves. Those who live immoral lives, who are idol worshipers, adulterers or homosexuals—will have no share in his kingdom" (1 Co 6:9-10, Living Bible;

see Lev 20:13). The Word could not be much clearer than that.

God's wrath is kindled against fornication, adultery, and homosexuality. His design from the beginning has been one man for one woman (see Gen 2:18-24). Jesus endorsed this divine arrangement as the only one acceptable to God (see Mt 19:3-6; Mk 10:2-9). Paul likewise followed the command of his Lord without the least change (see 1 Co 6:16; Eph 5:21-33). Man is never satisfied until he has tampered with every law made by God. This is because man himself wants to be god. And his misery stems from having to bear the awful responsibility of being his own god.

The family is not just the best social arrangement. No, it is God's idea. And that is why it is still the best and only way to survive socially, culturally, and morally. The basic unit is the family made up of a father, a mother, and one or more children. Some cultures exist today where polygamy is practiced. They have survived, but in a very primitive manner. Wherever the family is constructed on any basis other than the biblical pattern, there exists a deviant approach to the original design given by the Creator. For the preservation of society, the care and education of children, and the security of all people, the Judeo-Christian family unit is the only acceptable plan.

Sex must be contained within this family orb. Needless to say, sex can be abused even here. It can be the sole purpose of marriage and thus prostitute the family to a mere convenience for lust. Incest, a form of sexual existence strictly forbidden by the Lord in both the Old and New Testaments, also can arise among members of the unit (see Gen 19:30-38; Lev 20:11-21; 1 Co 5:1-2). No sexual intercourse is ever permitted except between one man and one woman within the marriage bond for life. This is God's plan, and anything else is man's making.

All departures from the biblical norm can be forgiven, but

the earthly consequences must be borne. And they are not at all happy or fulfilling arrangements. The ideal, therefore, is never to stray from the biblical concepts of proper sexuality in the first place.

My priority in the area of sex lies precisely within the biblical revelation. I choose to live as a married man who is meticulously faithful to one wife and dedicated to the care and training of our children. Any other approach to sex is foreign to my concept of God's will for His children and is repugnant to my mind.

Study Questions

1. Could the maze of deviant sex-styles which are coming to the attention of the public lately be due to a weariness with normal relationships due to sex saturation?
2. Will the family unit finally perish? If so, describe what you can foresee in its place.
3. Is there any justification for abortion? What is it? Who should make the decision? Or is a decision out of the question altogether?
4. What is a sex offender? Should he be punished? How should the courts handle matters of homosexuality and lesbianism? What should be the church's position in such matters?

13

All This – and Love, Too

LOVE IS A TRINITY. It takes at least three words to describe it. In some ways the ancient Greeks were wiser than we. At any rate, often they were more discriminating. They had three different terms to use in articulating the threefold concept of love. We have only one word, and it has come to mean everything from our feeling for country, friends, parents, a sexual partner, dogs, books, and baked potatoes to our feeling toward God. The Greek-speaking Christians never had this perplexing trouble with semantics. The three words they used for love were *agape*, *phileo* and *eros*.

Agape is the highest form of love that can be experienced or shared. It is a determined good will that has nothing to do with whether the person loved is worthy. It is a totally unselfish love which gives all for another. This love asks nothing in return. God's love for us is *agape*. *Phileo* is the affection felt by two friends for each other—a beautiful thing, but somehow dependent upon a reciprocating relationship which must move from both sides. *Eros* (the only one of the three words not used in the New Testament) may be said to be almost wholly concerned with sexual attractions. From this word comes our English term *erotic*, which is descriptive of a fleshly kind of love. This latter type is not necessarily evil, although it can easily become so.

The love about which I am talking is the highest kind of

all—*agape*. The love of friends has a place in it all, but even that needs to be exalted into *agape*. Some people think that erotic love is all there is—that this is what keeps things happy in the world. They are wrong. Our expression "make love" refers to this erotic sensation and clearly suggests that it is something that man is responsible for stirring up. The slogan, "make love, not war," speaks of erotic love. But this is not what will stop killing and hating. That is why our glib expression that love is the answer is destined to disappointment. Indeed, love is the answer, but it is a very special kind of love.

When Jesus preached love, it was *agape* that He was talking about. In answer to a lawyer's question about the greatest of all commandments, the Master said, "You shall love the Lord your God with all your heart, and with all your soul, and with all your mind. This is the great and foremost commandment. And a second is like it, You shall love your neighbor as yourself" (Mt 22:37-39, NASB); see Mk 12:30, 33; Lk 10:27). Talk about priority! There it is. Jesus says that this double-barreled love is *first*. But remember that the word He uses both times is *agape*! In the Sermon on the Mount, He goes on even further saying, "You have heard that it was said, 'You shall love your neighbor, and hate your enemy.' But I say to you, love your enemies, and pray for those who persecute you" (Mt 5:43-44, NASB). Obviously, neither *phileo* nor *eros* would work with an enemy. Only *agape*!

It needs to be noted that the master Teacher states emphatically that we must love our neighbors *as we love ourselves*. This, of course, cannot be selfish love. It is just the reverse. When a man has *agape* for himself, he does not do what gratifies his momentary whims. He lives in such a manner as to respect the life God has given him. He wills the best for himself, which involves rigorous discipline and continual inventory and chastisement. He seeks for that which will bring the greatest dividends in two worlds—for that which will fulfill the Creator's plan for his particular life. Thus, he must love his neighbor—even his enemy—in the same manner.

There is far too much talk today about solving the world's problems with "a little more love." The whole thing has a saccharine taste; it just is not real. Forcing legislation for equality, avoiding minority discrimination, stopping all wars, being nice to everybody, giving sexual tenderness to one who is lonely, accepting perversions as normal—these are not answers at all. They are usually drummed-up attitudes which really do not spring from a fount of *agape*, divine love, within our hearts. Love is not just permissiveness, commendation for anything that goes on, sentimental acceptance of another's activity when it is obvious that it is harmful to both himself and others around him.

Agape implies strength. It is not weak, nor is it afraid of truth. At its heart is truth, and that is why it is divine. That is why it is selfless, why it does whatever is necessary to express an *honest* good will. Of course, love accepts people as they are. But if it is *agape*, it does not condone anything in any person's life that militates against his final perfection in Christ. *Agape* is built on a long-range model which God has given us in His Son. It will never be approximated by anything less than a disciplining good will that is eager to love others with the whole counsel of God.

Sometimes *agape* hurts. If I have only a sentimental love for my son, I will be very careful to let him do as he pleases and never to hurt his feelings. But if my heart knows the love of God, it will be impossible for me to let him go his way when it is not right, and I will not spare his feelings when he needs discipline. If he has a thorn in his foot, I can refrain from touching it so as to cause pain, wrap it loosely, and kiss it tenderly. But if I love him, I will get a good grip on that foot and dig into the flesh until the thorn is removed—even if he cries. The latter is *agape*. The former may be what the world calls love, but ultimately it is something else altogether.

Agape sees to it that a man has what he needs, not just what he wants. A wealthy young man asked Jesus what he needed to do to inherit life, and the Lord told him to give away his riches and come and follow Him. He refused to comply with Christ's directive because he wanted what this world could offer (see Mt 19:16-22). But Jesus loved him too much to pamper his wishes. What he wanted was religious respectability. What he needed was a cross. Jesus was honest with him because He loved him. That is *agape*. If the Master had reasoned as many in our day, He would have told the rich young ruler that He was accepted without any need for change. But Jesus knew better than that. And He loved him far more than that.

Never in history has there been a body of people who loved one another more than did the early Christians. It so impressed the pagans that they are reported to have remarked of the Christian community, "Behold, how they love one another." But it was precisely because of that unsparing good will that they were so hard on each other. Reproof and discipline went hand in hand with acceptance. Jesus laid the ground rules Himself. "If thy brother shall trespass against thee, go and tell him his fault between thee and him alone: if he shall hear thee, thou hast gained thy brother. But if he will not hear thee, then take with thee one or two more, that in the mouth of two or three witnesses every word may be established. And if he shall neglect to hear them, tell it unto the church: but if he neglect to hear the church, let him be unto thee as an heathen man and a publican" (Mt 18:15-17). What the Lord was talking about in these words was genuine, realistic, eternal, down-to-earth *agape*.

No one has ever more beautifully and correctly exposed

the soul of *agape* than did Paul in writing to the mixed-up congregation at Corinth. The people had become confused over a number of unfortunate disorders which threatened the life of the church. Schism had broken the fellowship, shameful incest had created a sad image, quarreling and lawsuits had rocked the little group, some had continued to frequent the pagan temple of prostitution on the Acropolis, homosexuality was filtering into the church, and the Lord's Supper had been thrown into pandemonium by an excessive emphasis on and abuse of glossolalia (speaking in tongues—see chap. 3).

Specifically explaining that glossolalia is the least valuable of all the gifts of the Holy Spirit, Paul lists the varied spiritual abilities in the order of their importance. Then, in summary, he writes, "Try your best to have the more important of these gifts. First, however, let me tell you about something else that is better than any of them" (1 Co 12: 31, Living Bible). The section which follows is called "a more excellent way" in the King James Version and is a majestic portrayal of *agape* and what it does. This is the way *The Living Bible* paraphrases the core of this chapter.

> Love is very patient and kind, never jealous or envious, never boastful or proud, never haughty or selfish or rude. Love does not demand its own way. It is not irritable or touchy. It does not hold grudges and will hardly even notice when others do it wrong. It is never glad about injustice, but rejoices whenever truth wins out. If you love someone you will be loyal to him no matter what the cost. You will always believe in him, always expect the best of him, and always stand your ground in defending him (1 Co 13:4-7).

In this moving ode to love, the apostle compares *agape* to several gifts and fruits (they are not the same) of the Spirit—speaking in tongues, prophecy, faith, sacrifice, and martyrdom—and finds none of them to be above love. In conclusion, he exclaims exultantly, "There are three things that remain—faith, hope, and love—and the greatest of these is love" (1 Co 13:13, Living Bible). After all is said and done, only three qualities of the Christian life are eternal. Faith has the priority (it is mentioned first) but love has the preeminence.

Never has a better, more succinct summary of Christian living been found than is here revealed. Faith comes first in the Christian's life because it takes salvation as an accomplished fact on which none can improve. One has to start there. Christ has come, and His life becomes a reality through faith. Nothing can precede that, as was discussed in chapter four. Hope is a form of faith in that it grows out of saving belief. It is because I believe in what God has done in Christ that I have hope for the future. Having realized by faith that the Son of God *came*, I realize by hope that the Son of God is *coming*. Hope is grounded in the promise of the return of Christ and the perfection of His kingdom. Love is that disposition which literally bathes and controls one's existence from the realization which comes in faith to the actualization that comes by hope. From beginning to end, love is the overruling factor in the Christian's earthly life.

Even at the termination of earthly existence, these three dispositions will abide. When the gifts, so often put before these virtues, are gone forever, the trinity of faith, hope, and love will yet remain. They are eternal. Even so, love is still the greatest—not only above gifts, but above all other virtues as well.

How is this so? Gifts are temporary arrangements for doing a task in this life *only*. Virtues last forever, but only love is unchanging. In the world to come, faith will blossom into sight and hope into possession. But love? *Agape*? Love is the perfect state itself. It is divine. Love belongs to the essence of God. It does not see or possess; it is the final state toward which everything else is only a means. Love which is of God has not altered its true nature since the beginning. Nor will it be any different in heaven. Thus, *agape* is superior to everything.

All the priorities which have been discussed in this book must be tempered by love—strong, demanding, selfless good will. My personal priorities stand up to be counted in every department of my life. Not one of them can be denied or compromised. But overshadowing them all is that divine quality which pulls them all together and creates the harmony of Christian experience and service.

Love divine, all loves excelling,
Joy of heaven, to earth come down;
Fix in us Thy humble dwelling;
All Thy faithful mercies crown.
Jesus, Thou art all compassion,
Pure, unbounded love Thou art;
Visit us with Thy salvation;
Enter ev'ry trembling heart.

CHARLES WESLEY

STUDY QUESTIONS

1. Distinguish among the three kinds of love mentioned in this chapter. Illustrate each by thinking of someone you know.
2. When the Greeks remarked of the early Christians, "How they love one another," what did they see in that little community of faith? Do you think the world sees this in the church today? Why or why not?
3. Paul speaks in 1 Corinthians of "a more excellent way." More excellent than what? Why is love the way which excels?
4. Love is the perfect state, the divine fulfillment. Explain why this is so. Show how it is true that when everything else changes and even perishes, love remains precisely as it was from the beginning.